APPOINTMENT IN ABEREDWY

Y GOFEB

Mewn anghof ni chânt fod,
Wŷr y cledd, hir eu clod,
   Tra'r awel tros eu beddau chwŷth:
Y mae yng Nghymru fyrdd
O feddau ar y ffyrdd,
Yn balmant hyd yr hwn
   Y rhodia Rhyddid byth!

THE MEMORIAL

The soldiers of long ago
Shall not be forgotten
   While breezes cross their graves.
There are a myriad such graves
Beside the way in Wales,
A pavement along which always lies
   The path of freedom!

BY THE SAME AUTHOR
Marwolaeth Llywelyn ap Gruffudd – Y Gwirionedd 1987
The Ghosts on the Fairway – The army that vanished 1988

APPOINTMENT IN ABEREDWY

The death of Llywelyn ap Gruffudd
Prince of Wales

Anthony Edwards

Published by the author
Anthony Edwards
Hafodty Uchaf, Tregarth,
Gwynedd, LL57 4NT

Cover photograph:
Altar and screen, St Cewydd's church, Aberedw

ISBN 0 9514024 1 2

Printed by
GWASG DWYFOR
PEN-Y-GROES

CONTENTS

ILLUSTRATIONS

Photographs and map by the author except that *(p. 84)* of the bronze shield boss which is reprinted by courtesy of Royal Commission of Ancient Monuments Wales.

ACKNOWLEDGEMENTS

I am indebted to the following publications:

1282 – A collection of documents, National Library of Wales. Edited by Rhidian Griffiths.

Llywelyn ap Gruffudd – Tywysog Cymru, J. Beverley Smith, Gwasg Prifysgol Cymru, 1986.

Edward I, Michael Prestwick, Methuen, London, 1988.

Edward I, T.F. Tout, London, 1906.

Codi'r Hen Wlad yn ei Hôl, Hywel Teifi Edwards, Gwasg Gomer, 1989.

L'Administration Anglaise en Gasgogne sous Henry III et Edouard I 1254-1307, J.P. Trabut-Cussac, Libraire Droz S.A. Paris-Genève, 1972

The buildings of Wales – Powys, Richard Haslam, Penguin Books Ltd., 1979.

Llywelyn y Beirdd, Alan Llwyd, Cyhoeddiadau Barddas, 1984.

Permission to use copyright material has also been received from Mr Rhidian Griffiths, National Library of Wales; Professor Maldwyn Mills, University College of Wales, Aberystwyth; Gwasg Prifysgol Cymru, Cardiff; all of whom have given advice which was much appreciated. I am also grateful to Prof. J. Beverley Smith for checking and correcting my translations of his prose in my review of his work.

The Royal Commission on Ancient Monuments in Wales, Edleston House, Aberystwyth have also given me a great deal of help and advice, in particular drawing my attention to the paper by E.J.L. Cole, Vol. 21, *Radnorshire Society Transactions* and to the note in *Archaeologica Cambrensis* 1876, and for providing the photograph I have reprinted.

It is also my pleasure to record my gratitude to the Rev. John Hambidge, The Rectory, Aberedw for information about the church and locality and about the memories of prince Llywelyn which survive in the area today.

ANTHONY EDWARDS
Tregarth, 1992

INTRODUCTION

THE DEATH of Llywelyn ap Gruffudd brought grief and distress to his former subjects and the fact has been recorded in the fine elegy of Gruffudd ab yr Ynad Goch written shortly afterwards. This was an exercise in consolation and seldom can the task of the consoler have been more expertly performed. Firstly one must induce the mourner to display his grief, one cannot comfort someone who will not weep.

St Cewydd's church, Aberedw.
The altar displaying the Lord's prayer, the ten commandments and the Apostles' creed.

Secondly one must bring the mourner face to face with the realities of his loss, all the relevant facts must be clearly stated and accepted. Finally one must create a braver and more hopeful mood with which to face the future.

All these stages are evident in the elegy. The sorrow, quietly stated at first and then more clamorously and with less restraint, and the consequences of the loss, the lack of his protection and the exposure to the whims of a cruel and vengeful enemy. The deepest cause for grief, the dishonouring of his severed head, is first mentioned almost casually, then follow ten lines beginning with the word 'pen' (head) in which the message is hammered home. The last lines strike a fiercer and more optimistic note and end with a vision of Llywelyn, surrounded by his high spirited horsemen, riding off to claim his lands in paradise.

St Cewydd's church, Aberedw.
Looking towards the altar through the ancient screen of Radnorshire style.

Grief for the loss of Llywelyn is still felt by his countrymen which the passing centuries have done little to assuage. For this no blame can be attached to Gruffudd ab yr Ynad Goch. Part of the reason must be the uncertainty and mystery surrounding the circumstances of his death. There are two irreconcilable versions. One, let us call it the accepted version, that he was killed in a chance encounter near Cilmeri, and another that he was induced to walk into an ambush and was captured and beheaded near Aberedwy. The first is supported by most of the official records and the second depends very largely upon Welsh tradition. This essay is admittedly special pleading in support of the second version, which, the author feels, has not received its due consideration. These views may be right or wrong but the author would feel happier if they were fully considered and either confirmed or rejected.

The 14th century church of St Cewydd at Aberedw.

In the following pages the murder of Llywelyn ap Gruffudd in 1282 will be studied from this angle. From the very beginning the truth has been painful for too many people to permit an unobstructed path to the light of day. It can however be reconstructed by a careful assessment of the evidence that remains.

DRAMATIS PERSONAE – 1282

LLYWELYN AP GRUFFUDD, PRINCE OF WALES

He was aged ±55 and was noted for a serious and thoughtful demeanour. He had been foremost among the Welsh princes since 1257 and had married Eleanor de Montfort in 1278 who died giving birth to her first child, a daughter Gwenllian, in June 1282. He was drawn into rebellion against king Edward early in 1282 by the rashness of his brother Dafydd and by the widespread discontent aroused by the king's officials.

DAFYDD AP GRUFFUDD, LORD OF DENBIGH

Probably some seven years younger than Llywelyn, he had always been ambitious to rule in Gwynedd and was restless as a subordinate of Llywelyn whom he left to serve king Henry III in 1263 but left him in 1269 to serve Llywelyn once more. Restless again he plotted with Gruffudd ap Gwenwynwyn to murder Llywelyn in 1274 but the plot was discovered and he fled to England to join king Edward when he attacked Wales in 1277. He expected to be given Gwynedd but was only given the lordship of Denbigh and still unsatisfied he started a rebellion in 1282 in an attempt to wrest the Welsh leadership from Llywelyn.

GRUFFUDD AP GWENWYNWYN, RULER OF SOUTH POWYS

He was over 70 years of age in 1282. His father Gwenwynwyn had died when he was a child and he spent his youth in England up to about 30 years of age when he was reinstated in the family lands by king Henry III as the king's vassal. He married Hawys, sister of Roger Lestrange, who bore him several sons. They all joined actively in the war of 1282 on the king's side.

EDWARD, KING OF ENGLAND,
LORD OF IRELAND, DUKE OF AQUITAINE

He was aged 43 with a drooping left eyelid and spoke with a lisp. He was French by family and in speech, and was a very widely travelled man. He went to Spain in 1254 to marry a Spanish princess and made frequent lengthy visits to Gascony. The first three years of his reign were spent on crusade in the Middle East. He never set foot in Ireland.

JOHN PECKHAM, ARCHBISHOP OF CANTERBURY SINCE 1279

A scheming man, clever and scholarly, he was well informed in political matters. He was always ready to show deference to king Edward and when in conflict to retreat, often to jump all the better at a later date; he was by no means subordinate in church affairs owing to his strong allegiance to the Pope. He was wholly out of sympathy with the Welsh and strongly supported the king's policy in Wales, in all he was more than a match for the king. He distributed excommunications like confetti at a wedding.

ANIAN, BISHOP OF BANGOR SINCE 1267

Esgob ein heneidiau ni!
Pan nesao'r creulon flaidd,
I ddinistrio'r gorlan glyd –
Llarpio'r ŵyn a tharfu'r praidd –
Gwarchod ni rhag pob rhyw bla,
Gwylia drosom, Fugail da.

Pan fo'r cyflog-was yn ffoi,
  Gydag aur yn llanw'i fryd,
Pan na fyddo yno mwy
  Wyliwr dros y gorlan glyd,
Saf dy hunan yn y ddôr,
Cadw'r praidd, O Arglwydd Iôr.

Emynau'r Eglwys, 176*

He was a man whom it is kindest to call very cautious. On Palm Sunday 1277 on the outbreak of war, bishop Anian rose early and made ready for a long journey; he then read mass in his cathedral and finished by reading the excommunication of Llywelyn ap Gruffudd in Latin, after which he left hurriedly for England and in the end reached sanctuary in the Abbey of St Albans. He had been a member of Llywelyn's council and a trusted adviser but he opposed any resistance to king Edward in his war against Wales. After peace was restored he returned to Bangor but left again when war broke out in 1282 and joined the king at Rhuddlan.

ANIAN, BISHOP OF ST ASAPH SINCE 1268

Psalm 119 v. 161

Princes have persecuted me without a cause: but my heart standeth in awe of thy word.

A quarrelsome man but brave and resolute in defence of church interests. He worked amicably with Llywelyn until 1273 when he took king Edward's side in disputes with the Welsh and he supported the king in the war of 1277. When war broke out once more in 1282 there was local fighting between Welsh and English in Clwyd in the course of which Anian's cathedral was burnt down. He left his diocese in fury and refused to give king Edward any further support and refused to confirm the excommunication of the Welsh. The king then confiscated

*The Welsh version of the hymn 'Bishop of the souls of men' by G. Moultrie.

Anian's property and forbade his return to St Asaph when peace was restored.

MADOG AP CYNWRIG (MADOG MÎN), ARCHDEACON OF ANGLESEY

He would have been in charge of the diocese of Bangor after the flight of bishop Anian and would have had responsibility for Llywelyn's letters. There is a very old and well recorded tradition that he betrayed Llywelyn and induced him to make his ill-fated expedition to Builth.

ADDA AB YNYR (BRAWD ADDA O NANNAU)

He was a brother of bishop Anian of St Asaph and archbishop Peckham's chosen intermediary in his dialogue with Llywelyn in 1282. He was left in Gwynedd when John Peckham left, after which he would be reporting to Madog ap Cynwrig. During the day whose evening would bring Llywelyn's death John Peckham, by then at Sugwas on the river Wye, wrote to Adda recalling him from Gwynedd.

GRUFFUDD AB OWAIN, LORD OF ELFAEL UWCH MYNYDD

His territory could be described roughly as the southern half of the former county of Radnor. It had maintained a remarkable degree of independence until falling into the hands of Edmund Mortimer as escheat after Llywelyn's death. It had been under Llywelyn's rule since he established overlordship over Owain ap Maredudd in 1260, by 1282 Owain's place had been taken by his son Gruffudd.

THE MORTIMERS OF WIGMORE

The family had owned land in the Welsh Marches since the days of William the conqueror. Roger Mortimer, a few years younger than Llywelyn, was among the claimants to the lands of Llywelyn Fawr on the death of Dafydd ap Llywelyn in 1246. His mother was Gwladus Ddu, daughter of Llywelyn Fawr. For most of his life he was Llywelyn ap Gruffudd's rival as they struggled for dominance in central Wales, but in 1281 they were reconciled and signed a treaty of friendship and support at Radnor. In 1282 Roger Mortimer died leaving two sons, Edmund aged ±32 and Roger aged 26. Edmund was conscientious and had considered following a career in the church at one time. Roger was less conscientious.

MAUD LANGESPEY

She was a grand-daughter of Llywelyn Fawr through her mother Marged who had married Walter Clifford who owned wide estates in Wales and the Marches to which Maud was his sole heir. Her matrimonial affairs were complex and will be discussed below, but in 1282 she was the widow of William Langespey, Earl of Salisbury.

JOHN GIFFARD, CONSTANBLE OF BUILTH CASTLE IN 1282

A landowner in Shropshire and Gloucestershire who had been active in Welsh politics since the days of Simon de Montfort. In 1282 a body of soldiers recruited in Shropshire were under his command and given the task of defending the castle. He was a suitor for the hand of Maud Langespey, and had tried to marry her by force in 1271.

ROGER LESTRANGE, COMMANDING THE KING'S FORCES IN THE MARCH IN 1282

These included a small detachment from the king's personal bodyguard. He was the son of John Lestrange who owned land in Cheshire and Shropshire. His sister Hawys married Gruffudd ap Gwenwynwyn and took part in the plot to murder Llywelyn ap Gruffudd in 1274.

ROBERT BODY

He was one of the group involved in the ambush of Llywelyn, and came from Shropshire where he was given wide estates taken from their Welsh owners after Llywelyn's death.

STEPHEN DE FRANKTON

He was also from Shropshire and was probably among the group set to ambush Llywelyn. In the chronicle of Walter of Guisborough he is named as the man who killed him, and for many years this account has been accepted as authentic, but recently grave doubts have been expressed about its reliability. Stephen de Frankton does not appear to have been rewarded for his part in the death of Llywelyn.

THE EVIDENCE

A commentary on the National Library of Wales publication 1986
1282 – A collection of documents
Edited by Rhidian Griffiths

THE MYSTERY of the death of Llywelyn ap Gruffudd on Friday, December 11th 1282, and it still remains a mystery, is caused, not by lack of evidence, but by contradictions and implausibilities in the evidence that remains. There is in fact a very large amount of material, some wholly dependable and some wholly fictitious. A most careful assessment is needed by anyone in search of the truth.

To consider first the evidence that is of unquestionable accuracy. John Peckham, archbishop of Canterbury, had been in close touch with those involved in Llywelyn's death and knew exactly what had taken place. Six days later on Thursday, December 17th he wrote to king Edward to tell him what he knew. His letter has to be quoted in full. It was written in French and the English version comes from the source given above as is true for the other quotations.

> **To his very dear lord Edward, by the grace of God king of England, lord of Ireland, duke of Aquitaine, Friar John, by the grace of God, archbishop of Canterbury, primate of all England, greeting in great reverence. Lord, know that those who were at the death of Llywelyn found in the most secret part of his body some small things which we have seen. Among the other things there was a treasonable letter disguised by false names. And that you may be warned, we send a copy of the letter to the bishop of Bath, and the letter**

itself Edmund Mortimer has, with Llywelyn's privy seal, and these things you may have at your pleasure. And this we send to warn you, and not that any one should be troubled for it. And we pray you that no one may suffer death or mutilation in consequence of our information, and that what we send you may be secret. Besides this, lord, know that lady Maud Lungespey prayed us by letter to absolve Llywelyn, that he might be buried in consecrated ground, and we sent word to her that we would do nothing if it could not be proved that he showed signs of true repentance before his death. And Edmund Mortimer said to me that he had heard from his servants who were at the death that he asked for the priest before his death, but without sure certainty we will do nothing. Besides this, lord, know that the very day that he was killed, a white monk sang mass to him, and my lord Roger Mortimer has the vestments. Besides this, lord, we request you to take pity on clerks, that you will suffer no one to kill them nor do them bodily injury. And know, lord, God protect you from evil, if you do not prevent it according to your power, you fall into the sentence, for to suffer what one can prevent is the same as to consent. And, therefore, lord, we pray you that it may please you that the clerks who are in Snowdon may go thence and seek better things with their property in France or elsewhere. For because we believe that Snowdon will be yours, if it happen that in conquering or afterwards, harm is done to clerks, God will accuse you of it, and your good renown will be blemished, and we shall be considered cowardly. And of these things, lord, if it please you, send us your pleasure, for we will give thereto what counsel we can, either by going thither or by some other way. And know, lord, if you do not fulfil our prayer, you will put us in sadness which we shall never leave in this mortal life. Lord, God keep you, and all that belongs to you. This letter was written at Pembridge, Thursday after St. Lucy's day. *(p. 13)*

In spite of his deference to the king, John Peckham is by no means servile. Should the king treat the clergy harshly his archbishop threatens to become 'sad'. One feels that the king had previous experience of this 'sadness' and not enjoyed it.

A less informative but equally dependable account is contained in a letter to king Edward from Roger Lestrange, commander of the forces provided by the king.

> **To his most noble lord by the grace of God king of England, lord of Ireland and duke of Guyenne, Roger l'Estrange sends greeting, honour and reverence, if it please him: Know, lord, that your good men whom you assigned to me from your entourage fought with Llywelyn ap Gruffudd in the country of Builth on the Friday next after the feast of Saint Nicholas; so that Llywelyn ap Gruffudd is dead and his men discomfited and all the flower of his troops dead, as the bearer of this letter will tell you; and believe him concerning that which he will tell you from me.** *(p. 11)*

Next to be considered are the accounts given in the chronicles of that period. These were generally of monastic origin and were written some time after the events described, often many years later. They were intended for public information and therefore under more pressure to sanitise the record. Their accounts of Llywelyn's death are full of contradictions and implausabilities. An attempt has been made to distinguish the **credible passages** from the *incredible passages*. These represent the opinion of the author of this essay and not of the editors of the National Library's publication.

EXTRACT FROM BRUT Y TYWYSOGION – Peniarth MS 20 *(p. 19)*:

> **On Palm Sunday took place the breach between Llywelyn ap Gruffudd and Edward, king of England. And the autumn after that, the king and his host came to Rhuddlan. And he sent a fleet of ships to Anglesey, with Hywel ap Gruffudd ap Ednyfed as leader at their head; and they gained possession of Anglesey. And they desired to gain possession of Arfon. And then was made the bridge over the Menai; but the bridge broke under an excessive load, and countless numbers of the English were drowned, and others were slain. And then was effected the betrayal of Llywelyn in the belfry at Bangor by his own men. And then Llywelyn ap Gruffudd left Dafydd, his**

brother, guarding Gwynedd; and he himself and his host went to gain possession of Powys and Builth. And he gained possession as far as Llanganten. *And thereupon he sent his men and his steward to receive the homage of the men of Brycheiniog, and the prince was left with but a few men with him. And then Roger Mortimer and Gruffudd ap Gwenwynwyn, and with them the king's host, came upon them without warning;* **and then Llywelyn and his foremost men were slain on the day of Damasus the Pope, a fortnight to a day from Christmas day; and that day was a Friday.**

It is impossible to believe that Llywelyn sent the greater part of his army to receive the homage of the men of Brycheiniog leaving him undefended with the English army a few miles away. One must also ask by what possible route they intended to travel without engaging the enemy army. The strong impression is given that the chronicler reached a part of the story that had to be suppressed and, irritated at being forced to record an untruth, decided 'if they want a lie let them have a wopper that no one will believe'.

A record that is without obvious attempts to deceive is that of the Peterborough chronicle *(p. 10)*.

The Friday next before the feast of Saint Lucy, in the tenth year of the reign of king Edward, Llywelyn the prince of Wales came to the land of Roger Mortimer, in territory called Gwerthrynion, situated between an abbey of the Cistercian order called Cwm-hir and a town called 'Ynlanmake', with 160 horsemen and 7000 foot, to gain possession of the men of the said Roger Mortimer. And there came a garrison from Montgomery and Oswestry, namely lord Roger l'Estrange, the captain appointed by the king, lord John Giffard, *the three sons of lord Roger Mortimer, the two sons of lord Gruffudd Gwenwynwyn,* **lord John l'Estrange, lord Peter Corbet, lord Reginald fitzPeter, lord Ralph Basset of Drayton, lord Simon Basset of Sapcote, and lord Andrew le Esteleye, with all the might of the March of Wales. In the aforenamed place they met Llywelyn and his comrades at about evening time, and confounded him and all his army, so that he was killed in that**

same place; and his head was cut off and taken to the king at Rhuddlan, and from there was sent to London and placed on a tower. Not one of the prince's horsemen escaped death, and three thousand foot soldiers were killed; and three magnates from his territories died with him, namely, Almafan, who was lord of Llanbadarn Fawr, Rhys ap Gruffudd, who was steward of all the said prince's lands, and the third, it is thought, was Llywelyn Fychan, who was lord of Bromfield; whereas, it is said, none of the English was killed or wounded there.

The town of 'Ynlanmake' will at once be recognised by those familiar with the fate of Welsh names in English hands, it is Llanfair-ym-Muallt, after perhaps passing through a form such as 'Lanymiek'. It was Gruffudd ap Gwenwynwyn who had three sons and Roger Mortimer only two, but otherwise the account is difficult to fault. The date is correct, St Lucy's day is December 13th. The absence of casualties on the English side is confirmed in the letter from Roger Lestrange quoted above, who surely would have mentioned English losses if these had occurred.

The Hagnaby chronicle must also be quoted although it is less reliable *(p. 17)*.

After Epiphany **Roger Mortimer bade prince Llywelyn come to receive homage from himself and his men, and named the place; for lord Roger and other nobles of England had agreed that they should take Llywelyn by guile and kill him. And so when Llywelyn came with his men on the appointed day, apparently almost unarmed, his enemies rose up and attacked him.** *As the battle raged and drew on, very many fell on both sides. At length the Welsh were thrown into confusion and almost all killed, so that none was left save lord Llywelyn and his servant.*

The chronicler has incorrectly recorded the date, Epiphany is Juanuary 6th, but otherwise the first part is credible. Once again it is as though the chronicler reached a censored part of the narrative and continued inconsequently. The pitched battle arises suddenly although Llywelyn and his party are almost unarmed. From this point the account is impossible to reconcile with the certain testimony of John Peckham.

There are other chronicles from monastic sources that are relevant here.

Osney chronicle:

To please the king, thus did Edmund Mortimer and his brother Roger set a trap for Llywelyn.

Dunstable chronicle:

Thus was he treacherously invited to the March by the sons of Roger Mortimer.

A very interesting account is given in English verse by Robert Mannyng. Unlike the other chronicles there is no attempt to sanitise the story but the author has to be allowed his licence as a poet *(p. 15)*.

Llywelyn kept to the thickets of the wood, was craftily encamped at the edge of a quagmire. Sir Roger stationed himself close at hand, concealed from view with his bold retainers, and watched for the exact moment when (Llywelyn) should ride out. Llywelyn had no idea that he was about to be tricked and rode out with a few of his men to relax for a time. Sir Roger was aware of Llywelyn's movements, their banners swept to and fro until lord Llywelyn was captured. "Traitor," said Roger, "what good can fighting do you? Now that I have found you here, my labour seems worthwhile. Twice you have perjured yourself and twice broken your faith; twice you have been overcome, and then sued for peace. This is the third time you have offended (Edward) greatly. Accursed be anyone who speaks up for you, for you have been asking to be killed. Never in your life will you do any further harm to the English. Confess yourself quickly, for you must forfeit your head." Sir Robert Body, a knight whose sword cut best of all, promptly dismounted and cut off Llywelyn's head. Now Llywelyn's perjury is clear; his head smitten off; you may know that his heirs have forfeited their heritage.

The Sir Roger in this account would appear to be Roger Lestrange, and as Robert Body was one of the men under his command there would seem to be no further doubt. However Roger Mortimer was present at the scene of the ambush, as is given in several chronicles and is confirmed in the letter of John Peckham. Lestrange was in command of a garrison from Montgomery and Oswestry as well as a small detachment from the king's bodyguard and it is unlikely he would leave these, when Llywelyn's army was only a few miles away, to chase after a group of lightly armed men. This task would have been left to the group from the king's bodyguard, including Robert Body. The account is interesting for the description of the scene of the ambush, the fact that Llywelyn was tricked, the dialogue between Llywelyn and his captors and the suggestion that a priest was present to hear a confession. The words used by Robert Mannyng were 'hastily thee shrive'. It is also notworthy that there is a similar confusion between Roger Lestrange and Roger Mortimer in the Guisborough chronicle which places command of the king's forces in the hands of the twenty six year old Roger Mortimer.

THE CHRONICLE OF WALTER OF GUISBOROUGH *(p. 7, p. 8)*:
This is by far the most detailed account of Llywelyn'n death but unfortunately much of it suggests the 'dadleuon mân us' of Gwydion Gam*. The circumstantial details provided are too glib and garrulous to be convincing. His account is impossible to reconcile with the facts given by John Peckham in his letter to the king. The date he gives for the death is not very accurate, the feast of saint Nicholas may be November 13th or December 6th both of which are early. He also places command of the king's forces in the hands of Roger Mortimer instead of Roger Lestrange, but the most

*Gwydion Gam – the author of an apocryphal triad:

Tri pheth y sydd a fynegant anwiredd:	There are three signs of falsehood
anghysondeb,	inconsistency,
dadleuon mân us,	irrelevancies,
a thro ymaith rhag y gwirionedd.	and an avoidance of the truth.

serious criticism of his account is its close resemblance to the chronicler's own record of the battle of Stirling in 1297, he talks of the river Irfon as though it were as difficult to ford as the river Forth, and he quotes the actual words spoken by Llywelyn and these read like an echo of the dialogue between William Wallace and the emissaries of the English army before the battle. William Wallace was handy with his tongue and his cruelly wounding insults played a part in his victory, provoking an unwise attack on the strong positions of the Scottish army. The words quoted for Llywelyn are just empty boastfulness and few commanders would talk in such a way and few hearers would remember their words if they did. Walter of Guisborough's chronicle is full of good stories many of which have become part of historical folklore. Some of them are just a shade too good as though Walter did not like to spoil a good story for the sake of a little truth. In giving his account of Llywelyn's death he was undoubtedly playing to the gallery. It is a good story, well told and has become deservedly popular, but for searchers after truth – well, parts of it are excellent. The astonishing fact is that it has been accepted as a true and factual record by so many historians for so many years. This fact itself demands explanation.

Information of a different kind can be obtained from Welsh tradition. This tends to be disregarded by historians. Stories passed on by word of mouth can of course become garbled but at least they are free from the urge to suppress facts discreditable to their English rulers, which urge has distorted much of the English record. Shortly after Llywelyn's death elegies were composed by the bards. These were not intended to inform. Their elegies were recited to an audience who already knew the full truth. Information can only be gleaned by studying their comments on facts well known to both bard and audience. It seems expedient to consider this type of testimony after an attempt has been made to unravel the course of events.

A later record is shown on p. 25 of the National Library of Wales publication under the heading 'englynion traddodiadol'. The manuscript reproduced, LlGC 872D is dated 1590 and contains the following words:

> **'this was spoken to the servants of Llywelyn ap Gruffudd ap Llywelyn when they were washing in pistyll y geiniog near Prysgduon in Radnorshire, having fled after the slaying of their master at a place called Aberedwy at an assignment with a girl. He was the last prince in Wales.'**

Comments in a similar vein were used as heading to the elegy of Bleddyn Fardd on Llywelyn ap Gruffudd 'the last prince over Wales, who was killed in Builth through the treachery of Madog Mîn and others'. MS BL29 (Addl 14866)

There are other early references to th treachery of Madog Mîn, for example the cywydd of Llywelyn ap Gutun to the dean of Bangor, dating from 1480 or thereabouts.*

Finally attention must be drawn to a passage in Theophilus Jones' work titled *A History of the County of Brecknock* in two volumes 1805. The quotation is from Volume 1, page 139.

> *Llywelyn finding from their numbers that resistance would be vain, fled with his men to Builth, and in order to deceive the enemy, as there was then snow on the ground, he is said to have caused his horse's shoes to be reversed, but even this stratagem was discovered to them by a smith at Aberedwy, whose name as tradition says, was Madoc goch mîn mawr, or red haired wide mouthed Madoc.*

It is most unlikely that anyone fleeing for their life would waste time to get a blacksmith to perform an operation that would probably cripple their horse. Furthermore a horse in motion has considerable momentum and where the hooves

*Quoted in *Llywelyn y Beirdd*, Cyhoeddiadau Barddas, 1984.

touch the ground the soil (or snow) is driven forward so that the direction of motion is at once visible whether the horse is shod backwards, sideways or in the correct manner. The interesting feature of the narrative is the name of the archdeacon of Anglesey apparently taking sabbatical leave to work as a blacksmith at Aberedwy. Is this the last garbled version of an ancient tradition? Or is it a fiction intended purposely to deceive and to silence an embarrassing story about Madog Mîn, archdeacon of Anglesey?

Prysgduon in Radnorshire.
One of the earliest mentions of Aberedwy in connection with Llywelyn's death is contained in a tradition, recorded in 1590, of soldiers from the Welsh army escaping after their defeat and washing in a waterfall near Prysgduon and being reproved by the spirit of Gronw ab Ednyfed for failing to save Llywelyn.

THE ACCEPTED DOGMA

Llywelyn ap Gruffudd – Tywysog Cymru by J. Beverley Smith
(Gwasg Prifysgol Cymru, 1986)

A REVIEW

ALL WHO HONOUR the memory of Llywelyn ap Gruffudd must feel grateful to the author and publishers of this volume, the first authoritative biography of the prince. It contains an immense amount of information, studiously considered and presented with style and clarity, and perhaps best of all with a full index to lighten the task of the reader. What more is there to say? Well one point demands mention, not as hostile criticism but as an observation presented with diffidence. The account of Llywelyn's death in chapter IX ('Cilmeri') seems to leave much unsaid. The early records of the death of Llywelyn are contradictory and cannot all be true. The explanations fall roughly into two versions. Did he fall in a chance encounter near Cilmeri, or was he lured into an ambush at Aberedwy? J. Beverley Smith presents the evidence with scrupulous accuracy but it is the opinion of the author of this essay that the second version does not receive the investigation that is its due. There is a vision of Llywelyn falling on the field of battle fighting valiantly against a stronger enemy whose behaviour was honourable throughout. It is a consoling belief and one supported by a long line of eminent English historians and confirmed in several very early records. However, it is the purpose of this review to present a contrary opinion and to claim that Llywelyn died by treachery and deceit a long way from the field of battle.

The contradictions in the early records are so persistent that they give the impression of deliberate falsification. What were the motives behind this falsification? The atrocities of Richard de Clare (Strongbow) and William de Breos a century earlier have been recorded without a qualm, and the betrayal of Llywelyn, though more significant politically, was less of a problem for those pleading in mitigation. In 1301 king Edward invested his son as prince of Wales and no doubt made every effort to present him as a ruler worthy of popularity and loyalty who had gained his title with honour. In this context the deceitful and cowardly manner in which Llywelyn was killed was seen as an embarassment that had to be concealed. This tampering with the historical record must be condemned. We must learn from our past and how can we do so if the facts are sanitised and prettified to avoid causing distress?

On page 371 one reads the passage

> Mewn ymgais i esbonio dirgelwch . . . i'r traddodiadau gymysgu.
>
> In an attempt to explain the mystery of Llywelyn ap Gruffudd's last journey national tradition turns naturally enough to motives of deceit and treachery. The men of Builth were burdened with the charge of treachery long before the period of Llywelyn ap Gruffudd and perhaps the traditions became confused.

Certainly a humiliating defeat does tend to breed excuses but the evidence for the betrayal of Llywelyn depends primarily on the testimony of archbishop John Peckham and not on national tradition. Writing to the king he, as a trusted negotiator, would have no cause to modify the truth and would have been most unlikely to have done so. The men of the border country, throughout the whole of its length, were uncertain supporters of the Welsh cause at all times during Welsh history. This was inevitable in view of their vulnerability to English forces and pressure from hostage taking and the threat of devastation. The men of Builth were no exception and this same vulnerability was decisive at the time of Llywelyn's betrayal. There is no need to postulate a confusing of tradition.

Also on page 371 one reads:

> Yn wir, y mae rhai ffeithiau . . . yn gwbl rydd o faich amheuaeth.
>
> Indeed there are some facts which support the suspicion that the Mortimers, men among the prince's own kindred, were involved in Llywelyn's death. Their servants were hovering about his body immediately after he fell, and the archbishop revealed that an ambiguous letter taken from Llywelyn's pocket was in Edmund Mortimer's possession, and he feared that some English magnates were not wholly free from the burden of suspicion.

John Peckham writes that the Mortimers' servants were 'at the death' and he accepts their testimony that they heard him ask for 'the priest' before his death. Were they there before the moment of death or very soon after? This is an important difference. If they were there beforehand then the Guisborough chronicle's account of his death at the hands of someone who was unaware of his identity is completely discredited.

The 'letter of treason disguised by false names' is described by J. Beverley Smith as 'llythyr amwys' although the archbishop's words do not leave much ambiguity. English historians in the past have referred to this letter as a 'schedule'. Both the letter and its copy seem to have disappeared without trace so any knowledge of their contents must derive from the letters of John Peckham to the king and to his chancellor. However described this document holds the information that would solve the mystery of Llywelyn's death.

By far the most detailed and reliable evidence that is now available is that of John Peckham in his letter to the king written six days after the event by the king's trusted adviser. It is therefore disappointing to find that J. Beverley Smith only mentions it rather dismissively in a few words on page 371 and a footnote on page 372 and gives hardly any consideration to the contents. By contrast the English chronicles, some written many years later and all full of contradictions and inconsistencies, are quoted in wearisome detail. The Guisborough chronicle, which is impossible to reconcile with the facts given by John Peckham, and on which the author has himself brought forward evidence that casts doubt on its trustworthiness, is given two full pages 377-379. The Hagnaby chronicle is accorded a page and the section that gainsays John Peckham is quoted in detail in the original Latin. The Peterborough chronicle which agrees much better with John Peckham's letter and with the Welsh chronicles is dismissed in two and a half lines on page 381 and no mention is made of the absence of English casualties. This is confirmed in the letter to the king from Roger Lestrange, who surely would have mentioned English losses if these had occurred, and whose letter is dismissed in two lines. Understandably the controversial testimony demands the closest scrutiny but it was disappointing that the clues from the wholly reliable evidence seem to have been given less than their due regard.

The Welsh victory at Moel-y-don is turned into something of an atrocity and the English anger is recorded as so many prominent men lost their lives. It is difficult to feel much sympathy for these knights in shining armour, attacking unexpectedly during negotiations for peace, hoping for a pleasant day's sport hacking the lightly armed peasantry to bits, and finding that they were ill attired for swimming the Menai.

Gellir, yn ddiamau, . . . gellir rhoi cyfrif amdanynt. *(p. 373)*

One can certainly note that some churchmen who had served Llywelyn came through the war of 1282 unscathed and received promotion afterwards. But it would be extremely dangerous to stigmatise men like Iorwerth Foel or Madog ap Cynwrig, unless we have total certainty, with anything more than a readiness to submit to the order in the same way as did countless laymen.

John Peckham pleads urgently that the churchmen who served loyally under Llywelyn should escape death and mutilation and be allowed to face exile. One can plead that those who remained unmolested and afterwards received promotion at king Edward's hands should not be suspected of disloyalty to Llywelyn. Would John Peckham have agreed?

Diau iddo fynd â byddin sylweddol . . . ef ei hun. *(p. 375)*

He doubtless took a sizeable army with him, but the purpose of his journey, from a military standpoint, was to gain support in the borders from the Welsh community themselves. He did not go to subdue, but to gain a response and no one would would be able to do that but himself.

How large was the army that Llywelyn raised before leaving Gwynedd? J. Beverley Smith uses the term 'sylweddol' but for some reason previous historians have made effords to reduce the size of this army, perhaps to reduce the size of their later slaughter at the hands of Roger Lestrange. T.F. Tout states that Llywelyn 'escaped almost unattended from Snowdon before the winter snows compelled him to surrender' and later 'he soon reappeared in the Marches of the upper Wye hoping to raise a fresh revolt among the Welsh tenants of the Mortimers'. Tout was not sympathetic to the Welsh cause, in fact some of his epithets for Llywelyn (barbarian, shifty Welshman) might well have made him liable for prosecution under the Race Relations Act 1976. The Welsh chronicles state clearly that he left with his army to subdue Powys and Builth, probably with as large a force as he could muster while ensuring a reasonable garrison to guard Gwynedd. The Peterborough chronicle gives 7000 foot soldiers and 160 horsemen. J. Beverley Smth seems to reject the Welsh chronicles and to follow Tout in his view of Llywelyn's intentions.* But the offer of support from the Mortimers had presumably included that of their Welsh tenants and thus had been ensured before he left Gwynedd. What more was he expecting? He also chose to attack Builth before Powys and the inevitable conclusion is that he left to storm Giffard's castle with help from the Mortimers.

> Dichon na ddeuir byth at wraidd y gwir . . . i'w gyd-wladwyr yn yr ymdrech olaf un. *(p. 381)*
>
> Perhaps we will never have the full truth about the last day in the life of the prince of Wales. Was it a sudden chance encounter, or a long prepared stratagem? Was he a solitary fugitive, or a prince who fell with his army in battle? Among the princes in the line of Gwynedd he was the first for many generations to fall in the tumult of battle. Bleddyn Fardd describes him as 'A man who did not care to give way', and it would be well for us to visualise the last prince of Wales dying, as he lived, a worthy leader of his people in the final conflict.

There seems to be a suggestion here, as the writer of this essay understands the passage, that it would be seemly to give Llywelyn the benefit of the doubt and believe that he fell with his troops in battle and not as a solitary fugitive which would be discreditable. He does not consider the likelihood that Llywelyn was struck down by a blow from behind by one of Lestrange's swordsmen while he was being given an apparently friendly reception by the Mortimers.

The letter found on Llywelyn's body was described by John Peckham as a 'treasonable letter disguised by false

*Prof. J. Beverley Smith makes it clear that he does not follow T.F. Tout in his estimate of the size of the force accompanying Llywelyn.

names' and he goes on to plead that no one identified from the letter should be punished. Clearly he knew that the letter was of pretended treason and it is inconceivable that he should have said this if the writers of the letter were traitors indeed. It must have caused Llywelyn to journey to Builth to receive the support of those who pretended treason. Since letters were written and read out by priests in that age in all probability John Peckham knew of its existence before he came to handle it.

J. Beverley Smith nowhere mentions Llywelyn's privy seal that was found on his body. This unexpected find is of great significance. Why did he take it with him? To use a seal demands a document and to draw up a document requires a priest. Was there a priest among the party accompanying Llywelyn? There is evidence to suggest that there was. Quoting John Peckham 'Edmund Mortimer said to me that he had heard from his servants who were at the death that he asked for the priest before his death'. Note the definite article, and also note that if the servants heard him ask for the priest they must have been present before the death and witnessed the execution. Again John Peckham speaks of the white monk who sang mass to him the day he was killed, and that Roger Mortimer has the vestments. This is best explained by Roger Mortimer or his men putting to death a monk who was with Llywelyn's party.

Note also that Robert Mannyng quotes 'Sir Roger' as saying 'hastily thee shrive'. So a priest was present to hear a confession.

> Wedi'r frwydr deisyfodd . . . ddangos edifeirwch cyn marw. *(p. 383)*
>
> After the battle a relative of the prince interceded so that he might receive the privilege of burial as a true Christian, as he had shown repentance before death.

This is the only account that J. Beverley Smith gives of lady Maud Langespey's intercession for a christian burial. He never mentions her by name or gives her relationship to the Mortimers which was closer than that to Llywelyn, nor does he discuss the ambiguities of her marriage to John Giffard, the constable of Builth castle in 1282. Nor does he tell us that John Peckham had replied to her letter asking for absolution before he wrote to the king. The problems connected with this sequence of events will be discussed below.

For many years Aberedwy (nowadays Aberedw) has been accepted as the site of Llywelyn's ambush. Possibly the oldest record from 1590 is not mentioned by the author, nor are any of the subsequent ones. E.J.L. Cole's paper in Radnorshire Society Transactions 1951 assumes Aberedw as the site of Llywelyn's betrayal. The name Aberedw occurs only once in the volume, a footnote on page 419, where it is part of a passage of frothy rhetoric by an orator during the campaign of 1882 for a memorial to mark the spot of Llywelyn's death. The tradition associated with Aberedw has surely earned more careful attention.

Likewise one would have been grateful for a fuller account of the persistent and early Welsh tradition of the treachery of Madog ap Cynwrig.

These comments should not be taken as a lack of appreciation for an immensely valuable and scholarly work. It is of course impossible to please everyone and one is left hoping that some of these points will be investigated even if they prove to be false trails.

THE SEARCH FOR THE TRUTH

'Any nation that tries to repudiate history . . . only repudiates itself.'

George Bush, President of the United States of America
Babi Yar, 1st August 1991

THE OBSTACLE in the path of so many historians has been a reluctance to admit that Llywelyn was a victim of treachery and betrayal. A refusal to face this unwelcome but unavoidable fact is followed by a refusal to consider a vast amount of evidence that could lead on to the truth.

On John Peckham's testimony a letter of pretended treason was found on Llywelyn's body. When was it delivered to Llywelyn? It must have been delivered before he raised his army and set out on his last campaign. Who read the letter to him? The expected one would be the archdeacon of Anglesey, Madog Mîn, the senior cleric in the absence of bishop Anian. Thus the truth which so many people have been anxious to avoid for so long is as follows.

Shortly after the battle of Moel-y-don archdeacon Madog ap Cynwrig and Adda ab Ynyr read a letter to Llywelyn in the belfry at Bangor cathedral. It purported to come from a group of magnates in the southern Marches who offered to support Llywelyn in his rebellion against the king. These included the Mortimers who pretended a quarrel with John Giffard and asked for Llywelyn's help to attack the castle of Builth, of which John Giffard was constable, and if this task were completed successfully they would join him in an attack on Gruffudd ap Gwenwynwyn. As an added inducement they suggested lady Maud as a bride for Llywelyn and said she would meet him to discuss marriage.

The plot was in two stages. Firstly they would induce Llywelyn to come with his army to Builth, and secondly after he arrived they would detach him from his army and persuade him to walk into an ambush at Aberedwy. The plot was arranged at the instigation of king Edward but planned in detail by John Peckham and Roger Lestrange. Shortly after its successful completion they both wrote to the king at the first opportunity saying in effect 'haven't I been clever'. Lestrange was in command of the king's forces in the area and these included a small detachment of men from the king's personal bodyguard. During Llywelyn's approach to Builth he kept a careful watch on all his movements and reported these to the king. John Peckham meanwhile was in the area and on the day of the ambush

The Irfon ford and modern footbridge.

(Friday December 11th) he was at Sugwas on the Wye, but went on soon after to Pembridge.

Llywelyn's army was encamped that day at Rhosferig, a hill rising to a height of 700 ft a mile or so NE of Llanganten. Outposts would have kept watch at the Irfon ford (nowadays Rhosferig footbridge) and the river Wye would have given protection from the north. To reach his encampment his army would have crossed the Wye near Goytre wood where the river is fordable in several places. It is about a mile upstream from Rhosferig. Meanwhile the men under John Giffard would have been guarding the castle at Builth, while Lestrange's troops would have occupied the hilly ground south of the castle. The forces of the Mortimers and Gruffudd ap Gwenwynwyn would have been north of the river at Llanelwedd.

The river Wye near Goytre wood. One of several fordable places.

Sometime on Friday morning a monk of the Cistercian order sang mass to Llywelyn. It was saint Damasus' day. The abbey at Cwm Hir was Cistercian and had given support to Llywelyn's cause. At some stage that morning messengers arrived to persuade him to travel to Aberedwy that evening, lightly armed, to receive the homage of the Mortimers' men and that of Gruffudd ab Owain of Elfael uwch Mynydd, to plan a combined assault on Builth castle the following day and to meet lady Maud to discuss marriage. Having delivered their message, been well received and made the required arrangements the messengers would have reported this to Roger Lestrange. He could have sent his men on immediately to await Llywelyn's arrival, or he could have waited until Llywelyn

The river Wye upstream from Builth.
The river flows among rocks, and has deep pools and rapids. Further upstream the river has a wide flood plain and looks more mature; the site of a geological 'capture'.

was on his way and sent his men on afterwards. Both arrangements had certain disadvantages and it must have been a difficult choice. Some accounts of the ambush suggest that Llywelyn arrived first and others that Lestrange's men were there waiting for him. The intention was to separate Llywelyn from his army, to kill him and all his companions to prevent word getting back to the army which would be persuaded later to make a foredoomed attack on the castle. Lestrange's fear was that if word got back to the army it would withdraw to fight another day.

That evening, as the day was drawing to its close, Llywelyn set out with eighteen of his best men and a Cistercian monk to meet the Mortimers, Gruffudd ab Owain and lady Maud at Aberedwy. They would have crossed the Wye near Goytre wood and the Mortimers would have arranged a safe conduct for them past the troops at Llanelwedd which would have effectively ensured that they were cut off from their own army. John Giffard and Lestrange may well have watched them from the vantage of Builth castle. The Mortimers were at Aberedwy and no doubt kept up the pretence of friendship until they made sure that all Llywelyn's party were present. There was no other reason for the Mortimers to be at Aberedwy but the success of the plan depended on no word getting back to Llywelyn's army and if they were immediately attacked by Lestrange's men some might escape and carry back the news. While Llywelyn was conferring with the Mortimers he was struck down from behind by a sword stroke by one of Lestrange's men, a brief skirmish followed during which Llywelyn's party were killed except Llywelyn himself and the priest. Llywelyn was driven at sword point, weakening through loss of blood and the effects of his wound, uphill to Gruffudd ab Owain's dungeon (nowadays Llywelyn's cave) one mile away, to confine him while word was sent back to

Builth to ask for Lestrange's instructions. Llywelyn's cave is a strange dungeon-like structure with a narrow vertical door. In the sixth century it was the cell of saint Cewydd but early in the middle ages fortifications were built nearby and in Llywelyn's time it was part of the defences of Elfael uwch Mynydd in the hands of Gruffudd ab Owain.

Roger Lestrange's instructions, when these were received, commanded the immediate beheading of Llywelyn, and that the head should be brought to him at Builth. Llywelyn asked for the priest before he died and was granted a brief opportunity for confession. Llywelyn probably implored the priest to get word back to his army. The priest was also killed by Roger Mortimer or his men, possibly trying to escape. The beheading was done by Robert Body from Shropshire, Roger Mortimer kept the vestments of the priest

Saint Cewydd's cell, Gruffudd ab Owain's dungeon or Llywelyn's cave.
The cave as it appeared in 1988.

and his brother Edmund told John Peckham about them soon afterwards. The following day Llywelyn's army would have received a pretended command from him to attack the castle immediately. They would move down to the Irfon ford and while preparing to cross they would be confined to an area of about one hundred acres. They would then realise that they had been trapped, that Llywelyn was dead and the Mortimers hostile. They had come to Builth to give help to the Mortimers and had no reason to attack the castle themselves and no doubt realised that their situation was hopeless. The Peterborough chronicle records that Llywelyn's 160 horsemen were killed and 3000 footsoldiers with them while no one from the English army was killed or so much as wounded. This is confirmed in Roger Lestrange's letter to king Edward. He surely would have

The entrance to the cave in 1991, overgrown now and out of sight.

Interior of Llywelyn's cave, showing graffiti.
The location of the cave has always been difficult to find, but since it has become overgrown the task is almost impossible. Directions are given below.

LLYWELYN'S CAVE Nat. Grid Reference SO 08354685

The approach roads are narrow. It is recommended to leave cars in Aberedw and walk from there on, in all 1350 yards. There is a right of way.

Starting at Aberedw church, travel due E slightly downhill for 200 yards to a Y junction. Take the right hand road going downhill SE for 500 yards to a small bridge over the river Edw, on the far side of which is another Y junction. Again take the right hand lesser road going uphill SE for 100 yards. There is an iron gate on the right hand side of the road – please keep shut – leading to a track going steeply uphill due W for 250 yards, to an old quarry where the track doubles back to go SE again, slightly uphill for another 250 yards. There is another iron gate on the right hand side of the track at the foot of a low ridge. Llywelyn's cave is 50 yards W of this gate, behind a large caravan where a small wooden gate is seen leading to the cave.

mentioned English losses if they had occurred and he implies that the destruction of the Welsh army took place in a manner that was hard to believe. To explain this the Welsh army would have to have been persuaded to lay down their arms, probably with a promise of safe conduct afterwards.

In John Peckham's letter to the king he records that he had received a letter from lady Maud Langespey pleading for Llywelyn's absolution and then burial in consecrated ground, and he also says that he has sent word to her in reply. Where was the lady when all this was taking place? The task of pleading for mercy was usually delegated to the ladies and one might suggest that she was writing at the request of some other kinsman. The time scale for this is short: John Peckham wrote his letter on Thursday December 17th, six days after Llywelyn's death. His kinsmen in the area were the Mortimers who had already spoken to John Peckham in person and Edmund Mortimer had produced evidence to support absolution. John Peckham seems to have been well disposed to the plea but deemed it prudent to leave the final decision to the king. Since they had already spoken to John Peckham why should they ask lady Maud to write? If lady Maud had been at either of her residences, Bronllys or Clifford castles, she would have had to receive an account of the beheading from someone involved. She would have been fairly close to the archbishop who was at Sugwas on the 11th and at Pembridge soon after, but why should she wish to intervene? She was not very closely related to Llywelyn and would not have been expected to meet him often. She had a closer relationship to the Mortimers who had played the chief part in the ambush. Furthermore she had some kind of matrimonial bond with John Giffard, the constable of the castle that Llywelyn had marched to attack. John Giffard had put lady Maud through a marriage ceremony in 1271 against her will and in consequence was fined 300 marks to be paid to the king. In 1282 John Peckham still refers to her by the name of her first husband so he did not look upon her as married to John Giffard when he wrote to the king. Lady Maud and John Giffard regularised their marriage in due course and he gained control of her estates. Yet contrary to all expectations she felt distress after Llywelyn's death. Possibly she had been told that her name had been used to bait the trap but this should not have greatly disturbed her. A speculative suggestion is that she was with John Giffard in Builth and had seen, and perhaps helped to identify, his severed head when it reached him. This would explain her distress and help the task of fitting all the events into the six days available.

The Welsh tradition, recorded in 1590, states that Llywelyn was killed at Aberedwy keeping an appointment with a woman. He was in his mid fifties and unlikely to get involved in a casual sexual adventure. He had recently lost his wife and a marriage with lady Maud would have much to recommend it and it could have been used as a bait to get him to walk into the ambush.

King Edward's prior knowledge of the plot is certain. It is inconceiveable that the Mortimers and the other magnates involved would have dared to feign treason without the king's support. Furthermore the plot demanded cooperation between men while some enmity existed between them, the king's authority alone could compel this. When in October 1281 the treaty of friendship was signed between Llywelyn and Roger Mortimer (the father of Edmund and Roger) other questions must have been considered that the treaty did not mention. Assistance against Gruffudd ap Gwenwynwyn is an obvious example, but Llywelyn still held two castles in the Mortimers' territory. These were Aberedwy and Llechryd. The terms on which they were held must have been agreed. Again there was the question of the Mortimers' long-standing claim to the principality of Gwynedd. Llywelyn would probably have been prepared to support them in this should he die without an heir, discounting the claim of his brother Dafydd who had once plotted to kill him, had betrayed him on several occasions and had joined king Edward's army in the crucial war of 1277. Llywelyn probably regarded Edmund Mortimer as his heir. King Edward no doubt played on this treaty to control Edmund Mortimer – was it not treason? If he would join the plot he could be given Gwynedd. The treaty would make the pretended treason more credible.

The military aspects of the plot were in the hands of Roger Lestrange. It was he who arranged the disposition of forces in the March in the weeks before the ambush, he who kept Llywelyn under close observation and kept the king informed. It was he who commanded the detachment of men from the king's bodyguard who would be directly involved in the ambush.

How far was John Peckham, the archbishop of Canterbury, involved? He was in the vicinity of the ambush very soon after it occurred, talking to those directly responsible and copying the letter of pretended treason. The letter itself must have been written by a cleric so probably he knew of its existence before handling it, and have had a general idea of its contents. Why was Llywelyn carrying it with him? He may have been asked to hand it to the authors so that they could regain possession. The clergy were in a favourable position to gather and transmit information during a war owing to their literacy. They had unrivalled local knowledge and a nationwide network of institutions to exploit. Clergy took a key rôle in the plot, Anian Bangor, Adda ab Ynyr, Madog ap Cynwrig and who knows how many more. John Peckham's letter to the king strongly suggests complicity.* How did he know that the authors of the letter of treason were in fact innocent of treason? Why did he ask for it all to be kept secret? The whole intrigue

*As does the letter that John Peckham wrote to Adda ab Ynyr recalling him from Gwynedd, during the day before the ambush while he was at Sugwas on Wye. This suggests foreknowledge of the assassination.

was contrived with such subtlety, skill and ingenuity it is not easy to name anyone else with the adroitness to design it. Like many of the best plans it could so easily have worked in reverse. It would not need much change in circumstances for lady Maud to have greatly preferred to marry Llywelyn rather than John Giffard, or for the Mortimers to join enthusiastically in an attack on John Giffard and Gruffudd ap Gwenwynwyn. Gruffudd ab Owain would undoubtedly have chosen to fight for Llywelyn rather than the king, knowing full well that his days of rule in Elfael uwch Mynydd would not outlast Llywelyn. An everpresent danger was that the Mortimers' pretended rebellion would gain sympathy and perhaps support from their neighbours in the March who might lately have felt king Edward's heavy hand. Only one thing kept the whole contraption moving forward – that was the terror inspired by a tall Frenchman with a drooping left eyelid and a lisp.

KING EDWARD

A CHARACTER STUDY

WITH KING EDWARD'S conquest of Wales the dynasty of Rhodri Mawr, which had ruled the country for over three hundred years, was overthrown. During this period it had produced many illustrious rulers of whom any land might be proud, while the ruling dynasty in England had been overthrown twice, first by the Danes and later by the Normans. After his conquest king Edward became the absolute ruler of Wales. He differed in one important respect from all previous rulers: he was very seldom present in the land he was ruling. The day to day government was left in the hands of the king's appointed officials, and these were guided by the Statute of Wales, Rhuddlan 1284. This was a grandiose celebration of victory and like other of the king's works in Wales was inspired to some extent by vanity. The stately legal phrases concluded with a paragraph which enshrined the whole purpose and meaning of the statute.

> **And for that reason we command you to observe strictly the aforementioned in all things from now on, on condition that we can as often as and whensoever we like clarify, interpret, add to or take away from the aforesaid statutes and every part of them at our pleasure and as it seems expedient for our security and that of our aforesaid land.**

The king's instinct was to support his own officials on all occasions. Their desire for personal aggrandisement and essential lack of interest in the Welsh population they ruled were not a basis for good government. When Maredudd ap Rhys of Dryslwyn, who had a very long record of unshakeable loyalty to the English crown suffered at their hands, he had even travelled to France in 1286, where the king was at the time, to put his grievances. The king was sympathetic but did not over-ride his own officials. These followed a simple logic; Rhys was Welsh and therefore untrustworthy, his lifetime of loyalty to the English cause counted for nothing. In the next year Rhys was driven to rebel and later he was hung, drawn and quartered at York in 1292. One cannot shirk the conviction that king Edward's victories in Scotland and Wales would have had more lasting effect if he had devoted time to establish tolerable government in these countries. As it was he left this tedious chore to his officials while he went off on military adventures elsewhere, returning from time to time to crush the inevitable rebellion, the job he really enjoyed.

As a result of his hatchet job in Wales king Edward has become something of an 'English national hero', absurdly so because he was not English, nor was he 'national' in any sense of the word that would be understood nowadays, and his heroism depends very much on the direction from which it is viewed. An image of the king has been built up over the years with which we are all familiar. A strong wise ruler, fearlessly brave and uniformly successful in battle, honourable in all his dealings, a great lawgiver bringing Parliamentary rule, order and justice to all his subjects and forging a political unity for the British isles that can never be dissolved. The truth, as always, is more complex.

An account is given in the chronicle of Matthew Paris which describes an unprovoked attack by Edward (then aged about 18) and his followers on a young man who had an ear cut off and an eye gouged out at the command of prince Edward. It would be reassuring to believe that this act of wanton, adolescent cruelty showed a side of his character which he later outgrew. Sadly the evidence does not confirm this. Throughout his life he derived an irrational pleasure from dealing out death and mutilation. The letter of archbishop Peckham, quoted above, illustrates this. John Peckham, who knew him better than any man, feared that he would act in this way towards the priests in Wales who had discharged their religious duties under Llywelyn. It was king Edward who acquired a taste for the practice of hanging, drawing and quartering used for the execution of Dafydd ap Gruffudd, and later for those of Maredudd ap Rhys, William Wallace and others.

The reputation the king had for wanton mayhem was by no means a disadvantage in the time and place to which he was born. He enacted an impressive series of statutes during his reign, but his own attempts to interfere in the workings of the law were not rewarding. His talent was for law enforcement and the fear he inspired ensured success. Those involved in drafting the statutes thus could give their creativity full rein secure in the knowledge that the king could command obedience.

A rather similar situation arose during the building of the king's castles after the conquest of Wales. He deployed his fearsome authority to ensure that the building progressed while he was pleased to leave the design to James of St George, his master mason from Savoy, and others, many also from that country. The castles were planned on such a grand scale, far beyond any military requirement, that simple vanity must have inspired the work. Some were never completed and all fell gradually into dilapidation after king Edward's death. The most magnificent of them all, Caernarfon, was designed to resemble the walls of Constantinople on the Bosporus, a theme that reminded the king of his youthful years as a crusader. It failed miserably in its first test of war. This was during the rebellion of Madog ap Llywelyn in 1294, eleven years after the building began. The castle was the residence of Sir Roger Puleston, the heavy-handed sheriff of Anglesey. It fell at an early stage to Madog and the sheriff was put to death with a savagery that had been learnt from king Edward himself. The grandiose aspect of the castle is in marked contrast to the purely military and functional Rhuddlan. In spite of the massive stonework Caernarfon has something of the air of stage scenery, and the play acting rôle has clung to it over the centuries.

King Edward spent most of his life waging war. It was an occupation that he enjoyed; he was seldom at any personal risk or inconvenience and was usually accompanied by his wife. His children were born, as a result, in many strange places. It was an expensive hobby and the king was constantly short of money; towards the end of his reign the burden on his subjects, to provide for his needless warfare, made him unpopular. Very little that was of lasting benefit was achieved this way. He did indeed conquer Wales but left wounds that would compromise the English allegiance for the indefinite future. His Gascon mercenaries earned a fearsome reputation; to teach the Welsh a lesson he would let them loose to pillage, rape and murder to their pleasure, appearing himself later to restrain his bloodhounds and show that there were worse things than the rule of the English king. He tried to make the Welsh pay for the Welsh wars by taxing them at far higher rates than his English subjects. This ensured that the country was a powder keg liable to explode into revolt at short notice. His efforts to repeat his triumph in Scotland came to nothing and his campaigns in Flanders were abandoned at the time of the treaty of Montreuil when he made peace with France, acquired a French wife forty years his junior and arranged a marriage for his son with the French king's daughter which laid the foundations for the hundred years war. This was king Edward's legacy to his country, a century of useless conflict that achieved nothing in the end and was morally defeated by the inspiration of Joan of Arc, aged nineteen when burnt alive by his countrymen in 1431.

King Edward's prowess on the battlefield, for which he was rightly renowned, was learnt at an early age in the turmoil of the civil war, waged by the barons against his father Henry III, as it swept to and fro over the country. For a short while he had joined the side of the barons, but father and son were reconciled in 1261 and thereafter he fought resolutely on his father's side. The memory of this brief betrayal of his father, for whom he had respect and affection, seems to have soured his attitude to his own sons which varied between suspicion and indifference. He was a determined warrior who hated to yield and admit defeat, but he could be extremely cautious in starting hostilities. In 1256 he refused to attack Wales with the inadequate resources his father provided. At the battle of Kenilworth his great caution was the subject of hostile comment for many years afterwards. This was not cowardice so much as a heightened awareness of his own importance. He was conscious that wars can be won or lost very quickly by killing the man at the top.

Though he did well on the field of battle his success as a family man must be considered more open to doubt. He married his first wife, Eleanor of Castile, when he was fifteen and she twelve years old. Eleanor was a popular name in the royal families at the time, borne by his mother, aunt, cousin, wife and later by two of his daughters. From the time of his marriage he and his bride were almost constantly in each other's company, although it was seven years later that her first child was born. From then on it was parturition all the way until her death in her forties. The children were farmed out to be reared by other noble families and their parents, relieved of all responsibility, took little interest in them. The royal couple were in fact cuckoos, laying their eggs in other birds' nests, and like cuckoos they laid a great many eggs and faced a high mortality among their offspring. Again like cuckoos they never knew the achievement of rearing a brood. Eleanor of Castile was his youthful playmate, following him in all his wars, sharing in all his adventures but never really taking root anywhere. Her estates were run by stewards who were extremely unpopular, an unpopularity in which Eleanor shared and for which she must take some blame. There was a certain grasping acquisitiveness about her management that suggested the spoilt child.

In all she bore Edward at least fourteen children of whom five died as infants; five daughters lived to maturity but of his four sons only the last, Edward of Caernarfon, born when his mother was 42 years of age, lived to reach manhood. News of the death of his son John, aged five, and of his father Henry III reached him at the same time when he was in Sicily returning from his crusade. He astonished his hosts by being overcome by grief for the death of his father but indifferent to the death of his son. He explained that it was easy to beget another son but a father was irreplaceable. His son Henry sickened and died aged six at Guildford when the king and queen were in London: neither came to visit him. His son Alfonso died aged ten when the king was in Wales. Perhaps he looked on his sons as potential rivals, in the way he had challenged his father in 1261.

Eleanor died at Harby in Nottinghamshire in 1290 during November. She was aged about 48 and the king was planning a Scottish campaign. Her life up to this point had been devoted to the task of constant childbearing and it was six years since her last child, prince Edward, was born. Her daughter, Joan of Acre, born during her father's crusade, had recently been married at eighteen years of age to the duke of Gloucester, while her other four daughters were as yet unmarried. After Eleanor's death the king was grief-stricken. While carrying her corpse to London, he built twelve crosses wherever her cortège stopped. His taste for dismemberment did not spare his queen: her entrails were buried at Lincoln, her heart at Blackfriars and all that remained at Westminster Abbey. No previous king or queen had such an elaborate or magnificent series of monuments erected to their memory. One suspects that it was not only an expression of grief, great though that must have been, but that feelings of guilt reinforced the king's emotions. Not that he had neglected her or failed to provide every luxury for her comfort, not that he had not spent a great deal of his time in her company. In all of this king Edward had nothing to reproach himself. But all the same Eleanor had missed a great deal of the rewards that come the way of other women. She had never enjoyed the intimate companionship of a growing family, never comforted a daughter on her childbed, never kissed a grandchild, never quarrelled with a daughter-in-law. Her whole life had been devoted to the important task of bearing the king's children and that had come to an end.

One last aspect of king Edward's personality remains to be considered. It is a shameful chapter in history that one would prefer to avoid were it not for the light it throws on the king's character. During his reign he initiated a cruel and merciless persecution of the Jews in England and Gascony lasting rather more than the decade 1280-90. There was a religious and an economic aspect to the king's actions and one is forced to conclude that in neither of these matters was the king capable of rational thought. He was not, like Henry III his father, a fervently religious man, but he was devout in the religious observances expected of him and there was a strong element of superstition in his attitudes. This is testified in several accounts. The king's Jewish subjects suffered in his measures to stop coin clipping in the late 1270s and again in his attempts to suppress 'usury', the practice of lending money and charging interest. In that age Christians were forbidden to do that by canonical law.

Coin clipping is an ever-present danger where coins are made of precious metal and as the practice got out of hand the king tried to stop it by putting to death all found guilty of this act. The Jewish usurers, handling large amounts of coin, must at an early stage have been forced to do all their transactions by weight and may well have been the only subjects of the king who were not guilty of this practice. They were vulnerable to anyone with a grudge who might report them to the king's officials for sure enough large quantities of clipped coin would be found at their business premises. Many were put to death during this period.

The king's attempts to suppress usury were foredoomed to failure. The practice is in effect an arrangement to provide credit for commerce. Having forbidden the Jews to charge interest on loans, merchants were obtaining them all the same by offering indirect inducements. The king's belief was that a merchant who had to borrow money should obtain it from the Italian bankers who were dealers in bullion. This was no substitute for a loan with interest. Eventually the king ordered the expulsion of all Jews from England in 1290. During the expulsion they were at great danger from swindlers and highwaymen and many met their deaths on the road to exile.

The irony of the situation was that there was no man more in need of credit than the king himself. He always spent more money than he possessed. As credit vanished along with the Jews the king prudently decided to backtrack and ensured that some Jews remained – but they had to be baptised!

His oppression of the Jews in Gascony followed a different course and arose from other reasons. During the early months of 1287 when the king was in Gascony at Blanquefort near Bordeaux he fell seriously ill and made a vow that if he recovered he would go on crusade. The king recovered and duly took the cross but affairs of state made it impossible for him to go on crusade. He ordered the expulsion of the Jews from Gascony instead. Their goods and money were confiscated before they left but shortage of cash does not seem to have been the king's motive. Their plight was less desperate than that of the Jews in England for they could travel by land to districts ruled by the king of France and maintain their business contacts. When, inevitably, the king left for England they started to filter back and it is doubtful if the traders of Bordeaux were ever seriously inconvenienced. In 1294 king Edward was driven out of Gascony by Philip IV the king of France and when his authority was partly re-established in 1303 other matters claimed his attention for the remaining four years of his reign.

To explain the waywardness of king Edward's behaviour it is tempting to lay much of the blame on the heresy of the crusade. This was a 'holy war', an attempt to establish the rule of Christ on earth by means of the sword, in defiance of all scriptural commandments. Wars are in essence unholy, but if forced on us we should endeavour to make them as holy as practicable. The concept of a 'holy war' is an abomination.

THE TESTIMONY OF THE BARDS

THE SEARCH FOR CLUES IN THE CONTEMPORARY ELEGIES

THE STUDY of mediaeval Welsh poetry is an esoteric field into which the uninitiated trespass at their peril. However, the principles of common sense can usefully be applied to all branches of human learning and the message of the bards is too valuable to pass by. This testimony indeed has much to commend it; the elegies composed by Bleddyn Fardd and Gruffudd ab yr Ynad Goch were contemporary and free from any desire to hide or modify the truth but unfortunately they were not intended to be informative. They were celebrating facts well known to their audiences and deductions can only be made from their comments on some of these facts.

Did Llywelyn die on the field of battle or was he the victim of betrayal and trickery? The elegies are full of praise of Llywelyn's prowess in warfare but certain phrases seem to indicate that he did not fall in battle. Bleddyn Fardd 'Gŵr dig ei ddistryw' (a man whose destruction was violent), Gruffudd ab yr Ynad Goch 'Arglwydd llwydd cyn lladd y deunaw' (A lord victorious before the eighteen were killed). This states clearly that there were eighteen men with him when he was killed, an important fact that at once casts doubt on several passages in the English chronicles. Gruffudd ab yr Ynad Goch 'Gwae fi o'r aflwydd ei dramgwyddaw' (alas, for the misfortune of his downfall). The word 'tramgwydd' could simply mean physical stumbling but it could also be appropriate for a victim of deceit and treachery.

Michael Prestwick refers to Llywelyn (p. 19) rather patronisingly as 'a man of immense ambition and considerable ability'. What was this ambition? His intent was quite simply to unite the Welsh under one ruler to save them from subjugation. Consider this stanza from the elegy of Bleddyn Fardd.

Crist a ddaeth i'r byd rhag bod Addaf
A'i bobl yn uffern, gethern gaethaf,
I amlenwi nef, amgylch Naf uchel,
A golles angel anghelfyddaf.*

This seems to be an oblique way of referring to Llywelyn's desire to unite the Welsh under one ruler and again to the loss of independence due to Dafydd ap Gruffudd's lack of wisdom.

Gruffudd ab yr Ynad Goch 'Gorfynt hynt hyd Lydaw' (a path of conquest as far as Brittany) which has been quoted as a sign of Llywelyn's unbridled ambition, but it is nothing of the sort. When Llywelyn was extending his rule over the south of his principality some would have asked 'How much further does he intend to go?' and the humorous answer would have been 'as far as Brittany': after all, the Bretons spoke a British language.

How far was Dafydd ap Gruffudd responsible for the final catastrophe? Bleddyn Fardd certainly felt that Dafydd was to blame but that his heroism in the last months of his struggle and the grief inspired by the savagery of his death made one forget the anger his rashness aroused. Two elegies

*This can be translated: Christ came into the world because Adam and his people were held as wholly captive spirits in hell; to gather them around one high Lord in heaven that the least skillful of angels has lost.

to Dafydd carry this message. 'The pain of sorrow drives anger from my breast' and 'a man whose afflictions made me regret my anger'. Again, one elegy begins 'May God protect you from those poor souls in the fires of hell' and there follows a description of hell that could well be Wales under the rule of king Edward.

In the elegies to Llywelyn the words 'Llywelyn, hy y'i henwaf' occur with few exceptions. These can mean 'Llywelyn, boldly I will name him' or 'I will name bold Llywelyn'. Taking the first meaning it would seem that there had been some prohibition against speaking Llywelyn's name and that it needed courage to name it. Joseph P. Clancy favours the second interpretation. But Bleddyn Fardd, in his elegy to the three sons of Gruffudd ap Llywelyn, only applies this phrase to Llywelyn. Were not Owain and Dafydd also bold? Consider also this verse in his elegy to Llywelyn:

A berthyn am ddyn a ddywedaf:
A bortho gofid, bid bwyllocaf;
A fo gnaws achaws uchaf ei feddiant,
Ei feddwl bid leiaf.

Joseph P. Clancy gives a bland translation, perfectly correct but misty. The translation given below seems to express the bard's meaning better.

I want to speak about a man:
All who feel grief have got to be very careful;
If you have cause to complain, then the higher your authority,
The smaller had better be your intentions.

For purposes of effect the bard is making out that he is too cautious to mention Llywelyn's name. The previous verse and the one following also refer to Llywelyn in a very oblique way. The next verse, still without mentioning Llywelyn's name, speaks of him with unmistakeable clarity, and the one after contains the defiant words 'Llywelyn, hy y'i henwaf'. What was the point of all this if there was no threat against those who spoke his name?

From quite other evidence it would seem that Llywelyn was struck down and wounded by a blow from behind from one of Lestrange's men while being given an apparently friendly reception by the Mortimers, and that he was afterwards driven at sword point, weakening from his wound and loss of blood, a mile or so uphill to Gruffudd ab Owain's dungeon. This is how Gruffudd ab Yr Ynad Goch describes the incident:

> O gleddyfawd trwm tramgwydd arnaw,
> O gleddyfau hir yn ei ddiriaw,
> O glwyf am fy rhwyf ysy'n rhwyfaw,
> O glywed lludded llyw Bodfaew.*
> Cwbl o was a las o law – esgeraint
>   Cwbl fraint ei hynaint oedd ohonaw.

The last two lines have been rendered thus by Joseph P. Clancy:†

> Perfect the lad slain by hostile men's hands!
>   Perfect his fathers' honour in him!

Surely it must be better translated:

> A real soldier, with all the honour of his ancestry,
>   Has been killed at the hand of his enemies.

A man giving military service is not aways a young man: Llywelyn was in his mid fifties. If the bard had spoken in Joseph Clancy's manner one feels that he might have had his own head cut off – and serve him right!

* For the first four lines the following translation is suggested, including for clarity a previous phrase not quoted in Welsh.

> Lord Christ, may he protect me
> From the heavy sword stroke that felled him treacherously,
> From the long swords that drove him before them,
> From the wound to my prince by which I am riven,
> From hearing of the weakening of the lord of Bodfaew,

† From *1282 – A collection of documents*, National Library of Wales, 1986.

ELEANOR AND MAUD

THE INTENTION of this section is to take a brief respite from argumentation and to call to mind the two women who played a leading and tragic rôle in Llywelyn's life. The main facts are well known and have been described many times before.

In the case of Eleanor de Montfort and Llywelyn the story is one of surprising faithfulness between the two, which endured many years of separation, and was rewarded in the end by four years of married life. This was brought to an end by a late first pregnancy (she was 30 years old) and death on her childbed on the birth of her daughter Gwenllian.

Llywelyn's resolve to marry Eleanor must have been formed sometime in 1264 when her father, Simon de Montfort, ruled in England and Llywelyn was his ally in Wales. Eleanor was 13 years old at the time. The next year, after Simon was killed at the battle of Evesham, Eleanor and her mother returned to the family home in France. Her mother was Eleanor, countess of Leicester and a sister of king Henry III. When Eleanor became of marriageable age her mother pressed her to marry into the French aristocracy and certainly to find a husband, just as highly born, richer, more powerful and very much nearer than Llywelyn. But her daughter refused and remained faithful to Llywelyn, enduring the separation, the loneliness and the knowledge that she was growing old. How long she would have been able to resist is uncertain but her mother died in 1274 and the next year she was married to Llywelyn who, unable to be present, sent a proxy. She then set sail for Wales accompanied by her brother Amaury, a priest. King Edward managed to intercept the ship and imprisoned both Eleanor and her brother. Meanwhile the king was preparing for war against Wales and forced Llywelyn to submit in 1277. After peace was agreed at the treaty of Aberconwy, the king released Eleanor and arranged a marriage at Worcester cathedral and paid for the feast. This took place on the 13th October 1278. Certain aspects of the situation must have given the king much pleasure. It was unprecedented for a prince of Wales to marry under circumstances of this kind, and the bride he handed over was 27 and had endured several years of imprisonment with insufficient exercise. She must have been very unlike the 24 year old girl sailing to join her husband. Older now, certainly out of condition, possibly overweight but free at last to fulfil her destiny. Three years later she started her first pregnancy.

For Llywelyn it had meant long years without a wife or heir to his principality; it had meant enduring the insults of king Edward and in the end facing the bitterness of loss when he stood at her graveside at Llanfaes in Anglesey. All that remained of those long years of waiting, of the frustration, the anger, the grief and of the hopes that sustained them, was a frail little creature Gwenllian. She was less than twelve months old when she fell into the hands of king Edward who incarcerated her in the convent of Sempringham where she spent her life and died in 1337 having taken the vows of a nun 'of her own free will' when she was seven years of age.

Maud was his kinswoman for they both shared a grandfather, Llywelyn Fawr ab Iorwerth Drwyndwn, but whereas Llywelyn was descended from his grandfather's unmarried consort, Tangwystl daughter of Llywarch Goch of Rhos, Maud was descended from his second wife to whom he was lawfully wedded, Siwan (or Joan) the illegitimate daughter of king John of England. Llywelyn Fawr was the first prominent ruler of Gwynedd to marry into the French-speaking, Anglo-Norman aristocracy, but though Siwan proved a useful contact with the king of England she and her brood brought him and his dynasty little but trouble. She formed an adulterous liaison with William de Breos, who was caught in the act by Llywelyn in 1230 and hung a few days later. Siwan was imprisoned. Among Llywelyn's children by this union were two daughters, Gwladus Ddu and Marged. The former married Ralph Mortimer whose son Roger was Llywelyn ap Gruffudd's enemy for much of his life until their treaty of friendship in 1281, but the next generation of Mortimers plotted his murder in the following year. Marged, the younger daughter, married Walter Clifford as her second husband and Maud his daughter was his sole heir. Maud thus shared two grandparents with Roger Mortimer and was his full first cousin.

Maud, as a young girl, had married William Langespey, the son of an eminent soldier and crusader of the same name who was earl of Salisbury. Her husband met an accidental death in 1257. In 1271, John Giffard, then aged 39, had attempted to marry her by force and had been fined for this offence and made to pay 300 marks to the king. Maud evidently did not wish to marry him on that occasion. Eleven years later the archbishop of Canterbury, John Peckham, in his letter to the king in 1282, refers to her as Maud Langespey, so he apparently did not consider the forced union valid but the union seems to have been regularised soon after.

The estates of her father included land in Cardigan and Carmarthen but her main residences were at Clifford and Bronllys castles. It is unlikely that she met Llywelyn very often but she was a close neighbour of the Mortimers of Wigmore. It is not unreasonable to speculate that she may well have been present at Radnor in 1281 when Llywelyn and Roger Mortimer signed their treaty of friendship: she would have been an appropriate guest who was related to both of the signatories. Eleanor was then in the first weeks of her pregnancy and Llywelyn a happily married man. A year later when Llywelyn was a widower the suggestion was made of a marriage to Maud. She held out the promise, not only of the companionship of a wife, but of the help and support of the Anglo-Norman magnates of the March, without which Llywelyn's cause could hardly succeed. In 1282, during the long journey to Aberedwy, Maud must have seemed like the light at the end of a long dark tunnel. It was a light that Llywelyn was never to reach.

'BUT WHAT GOOD CAME OF IT AT LAST?'

'Why that I cannot tell,' said he
'But 'twas a famous victory.'

Robert Southey

ON 24TH APRIL 1284 queen Eleanor was delivered of a son in Caernarfon. He was called Edward. She was 42 years of age and this was to be her last child. Two previous sons, John and Henry, died as young children and a third, Alfonso, ten years old, was to die during the coming summer. Probably Caernarfon had been chosen for the queen's confinement because of the romantic associations of the place in legend and history. King Edward must have displayed the young prince proudly to his newly acquired Welsh subjects and he must have said something on that occasion. He certainly did not name him as prince of Wales and pass over the claims of his elder brother, and no doubt he intended to rule Wales himself for the immediate future. The likelihood is that he showed them his son, born in Wales and with no knowledge of French or English, and said 'eich dyn', an ambiguous comment, but appropriate whichever way you take it. The story of the Black Prince taking the motto 'ich dien' from John of Bohemia on the field of battle has been shown many times to have been a 17th century invention by William Camden. John of Bohemia's motto was 'Houmout' or 'High Mood', equivalent, say, to 'Here we go': the servile 'ich dien' would have had little or no appeal to the soldiers of that period.

It soon became apparent that king Edward could not rule Wales, Scotland and Gascony; and in 1294 he had to abandon Gascony to the French king Philip IV, but the latter soon found that he could not rule both Gascony and Flanders. In 1299 agreement was reached between the two kings leaving Scotland to the mercy of king Edward and Flanders to that of Philip IV. This arrangement was finally recorded in the treaty of Montreuil 1303 and part of the agreement was that the widower king Edward should marry Margaret the younger sister of Philip IV. Philip himself was thirty years younger than Edward and Margaret more than forty years younger, but king Edward took his conjugal rights seriously, possibly hoping to sire a king of both England and France, and two sons were born of the union, Thomas of Brotherton in 1300 and Edmund of Woodstock in 1301. A daughter Eleanor was born later but died as a child. Another marriage was arranged at this time between Isabella, Philip's daughter born 1292, and Edward of Caernarfon. It was a fateful marriage, solemnised in 1308, that provided an excuse for the futile hundred years war. Edward of Caernarfon's defects of character led to his wife leaving him in 1325 and sailing for France with her 13 year old son, the future king Edward III. Roger Mortimer, the son of Edmund Mortimer of Wigmore, had by this time escaped to France and became Isabella's lover. They returned to England in 1327 and received widespread support, including that of Thomas of Brotherton and Edmund of Woodstock. Isabella and Mortimer ruled the country as the regents for prince Edward from 1327 to 1330 during which Edward II was murdered at Berkeley castle. Edmund of Woodstock had credulously believed that Edward II was still alive and moved against Mortimer who imprisoned him and sentenced him to death. No executioner could be found to carry out the sentence, fearing reprisals on account of his high birth and the doubtful justice of the sentence. In the end a convicted criminal was persuaded to save his life by beheading Edmund. When prince Edward reached the age of 18 he assumed government, overthrew Mortimer and Isabella and had Mortimer executed in 1330.

Back to 1282, Edmund Mortimer of Wigmore had shown remorse after Llywelyn's death and had supported the plea for absolution and almost certainly cooperated in the burial of the corpse at Abbey Cwm Hir. Somehow or other he seems to have earned king Edward's displeasure. Perhaps he was too ready to assume the style of prince of Wales that had been promised him, and he received little reward for the key part he played in the plot against Llywelyn. However, he did gain Elfael uwch Mynydd, which came to him as escheat on Llywelyn's death and by 1285 one reads of him establishing his own vassals there in place of Gruffudd ab Owain. His younger brother Roger, unburdened by any conscience, became one of the king's most trusted supporters on the battlefields of Wales, Scotland and Gascony and was richly rewarded.

A horrible question mark hangs over Roger Mortimer's record concerning the death from drowning in the Dee of the young sons of Madog ap Gruffudd of Powys Fadog. These were Llywelyn and Owain whose guardian he was. This territory became part of the lordship of Chirk, granted to him in 1282, and their deaths were convenient. There is no question mark though over archbishop John Peckham's accusation of adultery with Margaret wife of Roger of Radnor and with others and of his casting into prison a chaplain who reproved him. Having supported king Edward loyally for many years he incurred the king's anger by quitting his army without leave while on a campaign in Scotland in 1303. His lands and chattels were seized by the king.

Meanwhile Roger, the son of his brother Edmund, was growing up and in 1306, aged nineteen, he was knighted along with other young nobles including Edward of Caernarfon. The following year the king died and his son, now Edward II, restored Roger Mortimer, the uncle, to favour and made him the king's justiciar for Wales, a post he held, with a few short intervals, from 1307 to 1321. Owing to the weak rule of Edward II this post amounted almost to a free hand in Wales. In 1321 both the Roger Mortimers moved against the king's favourite, Hugh Despenser, who was extending his power in the south. Edward II raised an army and defated them the following year and imprisoned both in the Tower of London, and it was there that the elder died in 1326 aged 70 after four years of severe captivity. The younger escaped after two years in prison and went to France where he was joined by Isabella, the king's wife, who shared his dislike of the Despensers. She took with her her ace of trumps, the young prince Edward. Together they returned and drove the king from his throne in 1327.

For three years, during which Isabella and Roger Mortimer were the young king's regents, Wales was governed by Roger Mortimer in complete control. The title he assumed was the Earl of March, a title favoured at a later date by Edward of York who duly became Edward IV on his accession. What sort of government dod the great great grandson of Llywelyn Fawr provide? His uncle, during his prominence, had shown no sympathy for the Welsh and he established and favoured non-Welsh settlers wherever possible. He drove the Welsh of Anglesey to revolt under Gruffudd Llwyd of Tregarnedd and ruthlessly suppressed them.

One of the first acts of the Earl of March was one of which his great great grandfather would have approved.

Llywelyn Bren, the highly respected lord of Senghennydd, had been deprived of his lands by Payn de Turberville and Hugh Despenser, the king's favourites, with the intention to settle English tenants upon them. He had been driven to rebel and had received much local support but when confronted by a much larger English army he nobly surrendered himself to his enemies rather than cause the slaughter of his supporters in a battle they were certain to lose. He was hung, drawn and quartered in Cardiff on the orders of Hugh Despenser. Roger Mortimer, as Earl of March, had Despenser executed and returned Llywelyn Bren's lands to his six sons. Apart from this act of justice, which was probably inspired mainly by a desire to take his revenge on Despenser, his rule in Wales was characterised by personal aggrandisement. He adopted a style of more than regal magnificence and indeed the country fared little better under his rule than it did under that of his uncle.

Back again to 1282, two men have been named as the killers of Llywelyn ap Gruffudd, Robert Body and Stephen de Frankton. Both were knights from Shropshire known to Roger Lestrange and it is likely that both were among the group, chosen from the king's entourage, to ambush and kill Llywelyn. After the act was completed Robert Body was given lands in Shropshire taken from their Welsh owners. There is no record of special awards to de Frankton so perhaps his rôle was less decisive, but it is quite possible, likely even, that both were involved. Perhaps Llywelyn was first struck down by de Frankton and later decapitated, as is told in the chronicle of Robert Mannyng, by Robert Body.

Robert Body took part in the siege and capture of Castell y Bere in 1283, and Stephen de Frankton in the fight against Rhys ap Maredudd in 1287.

WHO WAS TO BLAME?

Gan Dduw ni bo cwyn ddi-elw*
Cynddelw Brydydd Mawr

THE CONQUEST OF WALES at the hand of king Edward must have seemed, at the time, to be a total disaster – when all the Welsh were cast to the ground. For many generations afterwards the memory of the rule of the native princes, all descendants of Rhodri Mawr, appeared as a golden age, the inspiration for endless rebellions. But something, after all, was saved from the wreckage and the fact that Wales is still Welsh after more than seven centuries is another kind of victory, perhaps a more enduring one. It is easy to maintain a national identity in the context of isolation but to maintain one when this isolation has been broken down requires sterner virtues. Perhaps, in the future, as European integration proceeds and isolation for all is swept away, the lesson will prove to have been a valuable one.

When disaster strikes it is a moment to apportion blame; someone must have been at fault. With hindsight it is easy to blame Llywelyn ap Gruffudd for his folly in being duped by trickery in 1282. Were not king Edward, John Peckham and the Mortimers all behaving according to form? So what could he expect? There were not many choices open to him. He was facing a winter of food shortage and dwindling support from his own leaders while the enemy were

*Against God let there be no profitless complaining.

drawing reinforcements from far afield. The logic of the situation demanded that he should muster all his forces and stake all on a final thrust.

Should he attack Anglesey? It was strongly defended and easy to supply by sea; it had fallen quickly to the English armies at the start of the last two wars. Should he launch a direct attack on king Edward at Rhuddlan? This may well have been his best chance. The king's army was short of arms and provisions and in poor fighting spirit. This fact should have been known to Llywelyn if Anian Bangor had been feeding information in the right direction. And king Edward himself was there, the cause of all the trouble. If victory should have come his way, who knows, king Edward's head might have . . . never mind, it was only a dream. Men in danger and despair are easy to trick and will rashly seize a hand offerred in friendship, and that is what took place. The 'letter of treason disguised by false names' promised to solve all Llywelyn's problems – Welsh support in Maelienydd and Gwerthrynion, support from the Mortimers and other Anglo-Norman lords in the March and, yes, a noble lady to be his bride. Could he risk offending all of these? Could he believe that so many trusted counsellors were traitors? He was persuaded to march on Builth; it promised to be a clear way out of all his difficulties but it was an illusion: her marched to his own destruction. It is not easy to blame Llywelyn for acting on the advice then available to him. Perhaps in the end it did not make much difference to the final outcome of the war.

If blame is to be attached to Llywelyn it must be for quite another reason. His relationship with his three brothers must considered unsatisfactory: he never won loyal support from any of them. This is in marked contrast to king Edward who never had any cause to doubt his brother Edmund's fealty, although he was rather ineffective when deputising for king Edward on the battlefield. Edmund and Roger Mortimer seemed to live harmoniously enough, but points of dispute must have arisen at intervals. The two Rogers, Edmund's son and brother, worked closely together during the years of their ascendancy. Even the three sons of Gruffudd ap Gwenwynwyn: if they quarrelled, their quarrels never reached the history books.

Llywelyn kept his elder brother Owain a prisoner from the date of his defeat at Bryn Derwin to his forced reconciliation after the treaty of Aberconwy, a period of 22 years. Llywelyn regarded him as a lion too dangerous to be let out of his cage. Towards his youngest brother Rhodri he seemed indifferent and anxious to dismiss him from his mind. He agreed in 1272 to pay him 1000 marks to relinquish his claims in Gwynedd. Rhodri had difficulty in collecting this and it is probable that some remained unpaid at the time of Llywelyn's death. Towards Dafydd, his brother younger by some seven years, his attitude seems most perplexing. Dafydd and Owain were both taken prisoner by Llywelyn after the battle of Bryn Derwin, but Dafydd was released soon afterwards and served Llywelyn for seven years, but dissatisfied with his position, he left to serve king Henry III from 1263-1269 when, still dissatisfied, he returned to Llywelyn, was reconciled and given back his former possessions in Denbigh. Once back he plotted secretly with Gruffudd ap Gwenwynwyn to murder Llywelyn while keeping up a pretence of cordial relations with him. The plot was discovered and Dafydd and Gruffudd left hurriedly for England to serve king Edward in 1274, later joining the king's army against Llywelyn in 1277. After the king's victory he was awarded the lordship of Denbigh. Llywelyn proved ready at all times to forgive Dafydd even after his treachery and basic hostility had been displayed again and again.

Bleddyn Fardd in his elegies to Dafydd makes it quite clear that he blamed him for the final catastrophe and defeat in 1282. He also says that grief for his death made him forget his anger, and he pays tribute to his leadership during the last months of his life. Indeed in one matter Dafydd's skill was vastly superior to that of king Edward or of his brother Llywelyn: at the time of his capture at Abergwyngregyn he was surrounded by his two sons and seven daughers. Dafydd must have been a hard man to manage but if Llywelyn had found a satisfactory way to achieve this the course of history would have been very different.

For those who wish to blacken the character of Llywelyn the story of his dispute with Anian ab Ynyr, bishop of St Asaph will provide ample ammunition. He had been Llywelyn's adviser in the years before 1277. Subsequent events amply confirmed his loyalty to his Welsh fellow countrymen and his own personal courage. He strongly opposed any armed resistance to the English king. With hindsight it is easy to see the force of his argument: he understood, more clearly than Llywelyn, the vast military strength that the king could command. At the crucial moment he was engaged in a dispute with Llywelyn about church matters. Could Llywelyn have taken his advice if he had wanted to do so? He was under pressure from numbers of his subjects with experience of English rule to whom death in battle was the less of two evils when the alternative was a life of oppression.

One is left with a sense of the inexorable approach of armed conflict and defeat and the burden of bitter resistance for generations to come. A resistance that the passage of seven centuries has done nothing to decide.

THE MONUMENT AT CILMERI

Fy ngwlad! fy ngwlad! Pa hyd yr erys dy ofid!
Pa hyd daw gormes yn benfalch ar lwybrau dy ryddid!
Yn rhydd y meddyliodd y nef i ti gael aros;
Yn rhydd fel y dòn, a'r hâf, ac awel y llwydnos.

Elfed (Rev. H. Elvet Lewis)
o'r bryddest fuddugol Eisteddfod Aberhonddu 1889
'Llywelyn, Ein Llyw Olaf'

My Country! My Country! how long shall thy grief remain?
And freedom's path be trod by oppression's haughty train?
The heavens decreed that thy land should ever be free:
As free as the breeze of eve, the summer, or the sea.

English words by Francis Edwards MP *Radnor 1913*
translated from the poem awarded the prize at the
Brecon Eisteddfod 1889 'Llywelyn, our last leader'

ON THE BANKS OF THE IRFON, some three miles west of Builth, rises a monolith fifteen feet high of rough microdiorite from Trefor, Llŷn. This is Llywelyn's memorial. It is an empty tomb, or to give these memorials their usual name, it is a cenotaph. Unexpectedly the tomb which holds the remains of the body frequently has less emotional appeal and influence that the cenotaph which houses only the spirit. William Wallace was hung, drawn and quartered by king Edward and his mortal remains may be anywhere or everywhere but his cenotaph, crowning the hill overlooking the site of his most famous victory, bears eloquent testimony to his greatness.

The present memorial at Cilmeri was unveiled in June 1956, but an earlier monument, an obelisk of rock from

Llanelwedd, was erected some fifty years previously by Stanley Bligh, landowner of the estate of Cilmeri, at his own expense. A public appeal to raise the money had failed. Bligh was educated at Eton and Oxford and trained as a barrister and worked as such until he inherited the estate. He was ostensibly just another member of the English aristocracy but he was proud of the Welsh connections of his family and made many and varied contributions to the life of the country in which he lived. The failure of the first appeal is an unhappy memory. Welsh patriotism was viewed with suspicion then, and many believed that Aberedw was the place where Llywelyn was killed and others thought that Bligh was only trying to embellish his estate. Stanley Bligh was a gifted man, forward looking and often ahead of his times, and to him must go the honour of being the first to erect Llywelyn's cenotaph. The rock from

Cilmeri – Llywelyn's memorial.

Bligh's original obelisk remains incorporated in the present memorial.

The spot chosen was based on the account of Llywelyn's death in the Guisborough chronicle. This is now considered unreliable but the site never claimed to be more than a rough guess at the place of the tragedy. It is supremely appropriate as a location for Llywelyn's memorial, even though he did not die in the immediate vicinity. It was in this area that he spent his last day with his army encamped at Rhosferig. Sometime that day he heard mass sung by a Cistercian monk, sometime nearby he met a deputation from Elfael uwch Mynydd that persuaded him to travel to Aberedwy to a pre-arranged ambush. Somewhere nearby his army was largely destroyed. Few places are laden with such fateful associations. The memorial is well situated and worthy of Llywelyn and it is also a solemn reminder of

The entrance to the memorial.
The blocks from Stanley Bligh's obelisk are flanking the steps.

those countless thousands of Welsh soldiers who fell in the English wars.

When king Edward died more than three months were allowed to pass before his funeral service was held and his body laid to rest in its unusual tomb, raised above ground level, in Westminster Abbey. During these months the attempt to subdue the Scots was abandoned, and the king's body travelled slowly south to London. On the way vigils

Llywelyn's grave in the former Cistercian abbey at Cwm Hir.
The abbey was founded by Cadwallon ap Madog of Maelienydd in 1176 on this site, and it was further endowed by his son Hywel and grandson Maredudd ap Maelgwn.

were kept and frequent masses said for his soul. For several centuries afterwards candles were kept burning around his tomb, but eventually interest was lost and the practice was abandoned. Today the tomb is just part of the attractions Westminster Abbey holds for visitors. In 1774 the tomb was the target for some unseemly inquisitiveness. A number of learned gentlemen, including the dean of Westminster, allowed their curiosity to get the better of them and they opened the tomb to have a look inside. There was the king's body, sumptuously dressed, and in fair condition considering the passage of nearly five hundred years. King Edward's body was in one piece at the time of his entombment but when the tomb was opened he nearly lost a finger to one antiquary who was looking for a souvenir.

By contrast Llywelyn's body was subjected to all the insults the king could command. His severed head was paraded through London, stuck on a pole, and was placed afterwards outside the Tower of London where it remained for many years. There is an interesting possibility that it may still be in the Tower, a jealously guarded secret. The king did all he could to deny Llywelyn a christian burial, although John Peckham had indicated that he was disposed to absolve him. Edmund Mortimer had spoken to John Peckham and given evidence to support absolution and he had probably agreed with Gruffudd ab Owain to leave the body for a while in the dungeon at Aberedwy. There is no clear evidence of what happened next but news of some sort reached John Peckham to the effect that Llywelyn had been buried at Abbey Cwm Hir. John Peckham clearly thought that this should not have been done without his permission, and he wrote twice to the archdeacon of Brecon asking if this were true. The probability is that Llywelyn was in fact buried there, at least John Peckham thought so, but this could not have been done without the knowledge and cooperation of Edmund Mortimer.

Llywelyn was publicly dishonoured and efforts were made to erase all recollection of him, but none the less his memory was kept alive in Wales owing to the harshness and corruption of English rule. Thoughts returned nostalgically to Llywelyn's days, to his grandfather's and to other more distant members of the dynasty of Rhodri Mawr. The advent of the Tudors, themselves descended from Rhodri Mawr through Gwenllian the wife of Ednyfed Fychan and daughter of Rhys ap Gruffudd, Yr Arglwydd Rhys o Ddeheubarth, mitigated the worst of the oppression. Other turmoils arose to turn thoughts in other directions. In recent years Llywelyn's command of popular esteem has grown while that of king Edward has waned. The final verdict of history can be very ironic.

The ruins of the abbey looking west, showing the outlines of the nave, the great hall, once the pride of the order.

NOTE ON THE CISTERCIAN ABBEY OF CWM HIR

The foundation (or re-foundation) of the abbey on its present site on the 1st August 1176 by Cadwallon ap Madog is well testified but there is a likelihood that there was a previous foundation for the order by Maredudd ap Madog, lord of Maelienydd, in 1143 at Tŷ Faenor, a mile to the east of the present site. Maelienydd fell into the hands of the Anglo-Normans in 1144 and the new foundation seems to have been obliterated. The Norman oppression continued, mostly at the hands of the Mortimers, who caused the death of Cadwallon and several of his brothers, and by early in the 13th century the abbey had fallen into their hands. Welsh control was re-established by Llywelyn Fawr and later by Llywelyn ap Gruffudd. After 1282 the Mortimers regained control and the abbey was sacked by Owain Glyndŵr in 1401 during an attack on the Mortimers. By the time of the dissolution of the monasteries in 1536 it had become impoverished and in 1538 it passed into secular ownership, since when its history has been one of spoliation. The finest remains were incorporated into Llanidloes church in 1542 and some carved stonework has been used in the construction of Cwm Hir Hall. A little crumbling and dangerous masonry remains on the site today to remind one of a building of exceptional splendour. What of the future? At the present rate of dilapitation final oblivion cannot long be delayed. Ominously at Tŷ Faenor, the site of the original foundation, the 1000 ft contours on either side of the valley are only 700 yards apart: a dam here could create a lake two miles or more long. The catchment area is too small for it to be of much interest to the Water Board, but for recreational uses it would do nicely! Llywelyn's tombstone could easily be lifted up and re-sited at the water's edge. Is this what we want? Well it is what we will get if we let things drift.

ABEREDW

WE HAVE REACHED ABEREDWY. Nowadays it is called Aberedw and it has been pronounced in that way for a very long time, by some at least. In 1293 the name appears in a legal document as 'Aberedou' and in another later the same year as 'veynor Apredou'. The association with the death of Llywelyn lives very strongly here today. The trouble with this tradition is that if Llywelyn was killed at Aberedw, a long way from his army, he must have been a victim of deceit and treachery and this fact has been distasteful to English historians from the very beginning. Efforts have been made, and still are being made, to say that he died on the field of battle with honourable behaviour on both sides, and this in spite of the clearest evidence to the contrary. For these people Aberedw is unmentionable.

In the sixth century saint Cewydd* lived here and used as his cell the rocky cavity known today as Llywelyn's cave. It lies about a mile south east of the present village. His influence was widespread in southern and eastern Wales and his name appears in several place names. In that age the 'saints' were not only the priests, but the schoolmasters, the doctors and the social workers for the community they

*St Cewydd is not included in the Church in Wales list of saints. His feast day has been celebrated on July 15th, 6th or 2nd.

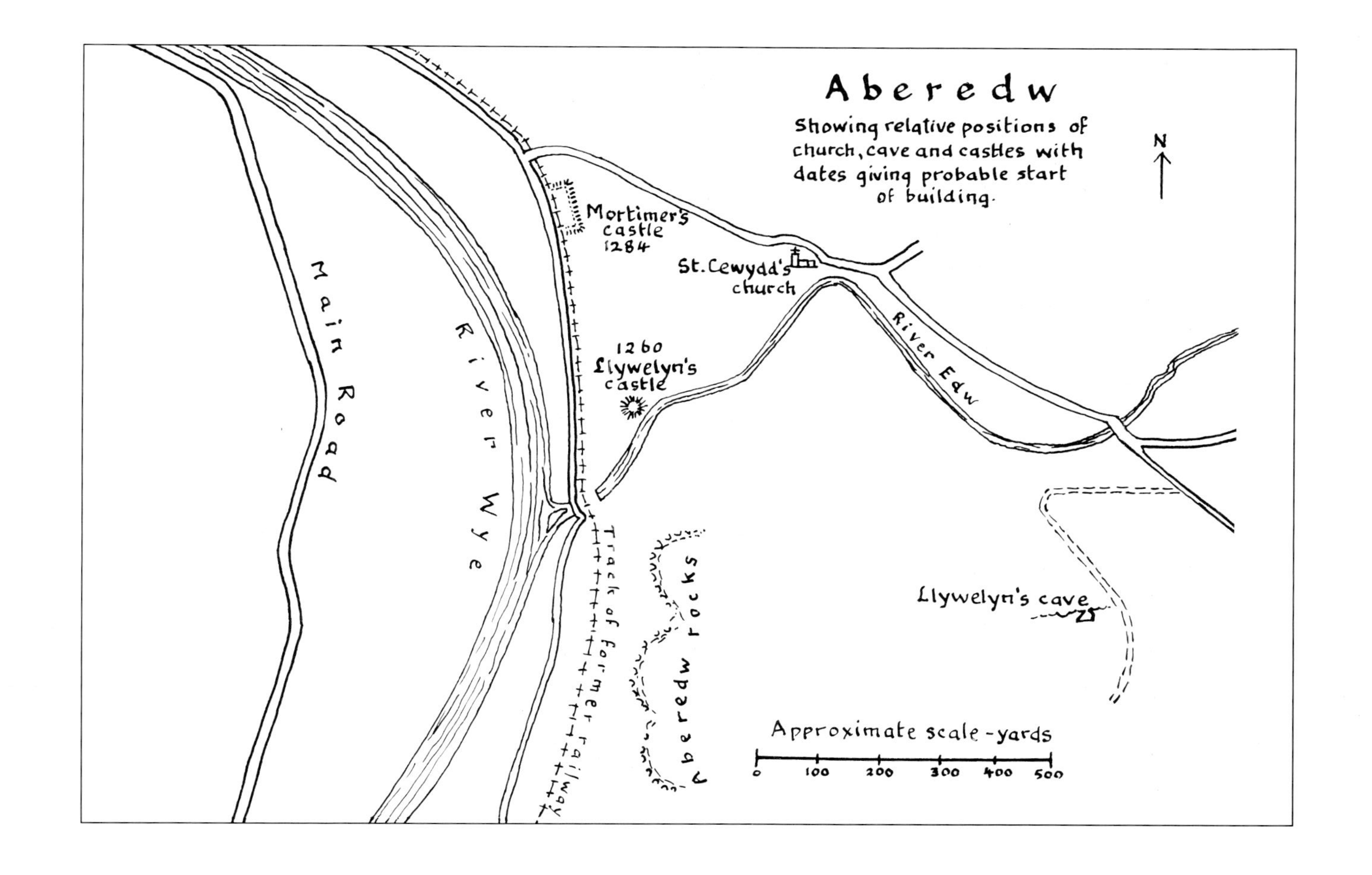
Aberedw
Showing relative positions of church, cave and castles with dates giving probable start of building.
N
Mortimer's castle 1284
St. Cewydd's church
1260 Llywelyn's castle
River Edw
Main Road
River Wye
Track of former railway
Aberedw rocks
Llywelyn's cave
Approximate scale-yards
0 100 200 300 400 500

served. He must have held public worship somewhere nearby and would probably not have asked his congregants to walk uphill to his cell. The chosen spot would have been somewhere near the junction of the Edw and Wye valleys, and could well have been close to the site of the present church, which is dedicated to him, and has been in use since the fourteenth century at least.

In the early middle ages the area was on the border between Upper and Lower Elfael and fortifications were constructed. It is believed that a Norman castle was built on the rocks above Llywelyn's cave which was used as a dungeon. Llywelyn ap Gruffudd in 1260 established overlordship over Upper Elfael, then held by Owain ap Maredudd, and built a small castle near the confluence of the rivers Edwy and Wye. The area passed to Edmund Mortimer as escheat on Llywelyn's death and he started building a castle for his vassal Walter Hackluyt some 300 yards to the north west of Llywelyn's castle. The sites of both these structures are visible but little remains of them today.

Bronze shield boss found near Llywelyn's cave in 1874.

In 1874 a bronze disc, four inches wide, was found near Llywelyn's cave and formed the subject for a note in the journal of Archaeologia Cambrensis two years later. It was identified as a shield boss and has been dated to refer to the fifteenth century, which if correct would connect it to Owain Glyndŵr rather than Llywelyn. It had four rivet holes through which it could be attached to a wooden shield, wielded by a foot soldier. While fending a blow the rivets failed and the boss came adrift. Around the centre of the boss appears a motto in Norman French bearing the gnomic words 'Nul bien sans l'poyne ou faveur' which may mean 'possessions bring pain or pleasure' perhaps expressing the view that 'every silver lining has a cloud' or that it is a 'good wind that blows nobody any ill', a familiar idea usually seen from another angle.

The modern village of Aberedw is a delightful place with a charm of a rather mysterious kind. The Wye valley here is remarkable; it is narrow and steep sided in a way that does not match the large volume of water carried by the river. In distant ages the Wye must have stolen the head waters of the river Tywi and as a consequence the tributaries of the Wye here fall steeply into the valley, often through wooded dingles. Aberedw village is difficult to see all at once or from a distance. It is a secret place. The river Edw is close at hand, seldom seen but often heard. Even the church can be missed by strangers but will richly reward those who visit it. The building is of great beauty and antiquity and has not been spoilt by later additions. The ancient screen of traditional Radnorshire design is most impressive and the fine porch, large and used as an assembly room in the past, is one to remember.

There is a local tradition that Llywelyn made his last communion at Aberedw church. It is just the type of story to evoke a superior, dismissive smile from professional historians. But there is nothing impossible about the belief, nor even unlikely. Llywelyn was almost certainly accompanied by a priest and if he had time on his hands what better use of it could be made? The possibility depends on one fact. When news was brought to Roger Lestrange at Builth that Llywelyn intended to keep his appointment at Aberedwy he could have sent the detachment of men detailed for the ambush on there immediately to await his arrival or he could wait until he was on his way and then send his men to follow him. Both plans have disadvantages. I have favoured the first alternative but the records are equivocal and there is not much to chose between them. Llywelyn could not have received communion after his capture because he had been excommunicated.

The linking of Aberedwy with Llywelyn's death is far too powerful a tradition to be dismissed by turning a blind eye. Those who wish to discount the belief should at least consider the evidence. What were the origins of this belief? When did they arise and why? What were the motives for this invention, if invention it was? There is one certain way for the whole matter to be cleared up once and for all, yes, the 'letter of treason disguised by false names'. Have the two texts of such an interesting letter really been destroyed? Has any serious attempt been made by historians to look for them? These questions remain unanswered.

Life was hard in the thirteenth century: murder and sudden death were all around. Should one fix so much attention on one death among so many? The death of Llywelyn was one of those incidents that decide the course of history; it was a threshold once crossed, once the door behind slams shut, that determines the destiny of man. The relations between England and Wales were now settled. There would be no more treaties of Montgomery.

When the severed head of Llywelyn reached the king at Rhuddlan, a week or so before Christmas, he knew his problems were over. Triumph would be his. It must have been a wonderful Christmas present! The conquest of Wales was to be king Edward's one undoubted success. Of course there was a price to be paid but that could wait; nearer at hand would be his triumphal tour of Wales and the Statute of Wales, Rhuddlan. This one brief moment was to impel the king's most loyal servant in Wales, 'Rhys ap Maredudd', relentlessly forward to be hung, drawn and quartered at York. It was to seal the fate of Sir Roger Puleston and his savage death when the king's grandiose castle at Caernarfon fell in its first taste of war. It was to unleash the king's Gascon mercenaries to an orgy of pillage, murder and rape in conquered Snowdon. At that moment it lined up in the wings the nineteen accident prone English princes of Wales, all as yet unborn, waiting for their cue to appear on stage. Glory can be purchased at a price.

*NVL*BIEN*SANS*L*POYNE*OV*FAVEVR*

INDEX